RICKMANSWORTH SCHOOL

FIFTY GOLDEN YEARS

On the Occasion of the School's Golden Jubilee, 2003

An illustrated and historical recollection of life at
Rickmansworth School between 1953 and 2003

By

Chris Morton
(1953 – 1960)

With forewords by

Patricia, Countess Mountbatten of Burma CBE, CD, JP, DL

and

Dr Stephen Burton MA PhD
The Headmaster

Published by Chris Morton

First published in Great Britain in 2004
By Chris Morton
willowgrayowl@aol.com

Chris Morton asserts the moral right to
be identified as the author of this work

Copyright ©CJM 2004

All rights reserved. No part of this publication
may be reproduced, stored in a retrieval system
or transmitted, in any form or by any means electronic,
mechanical, photocopying recording or otherwise,
without the prior permission of the copyright owner.

A catalogue record for this book
is available from the British Library

ISBN 0-9548755-0-8

Printed and bound in Great Britain by:
Doppler Press
5 Wates Way
Brentwood
Essex CM15 9TB

Ode to Ricky Grammar

Up Scot's Hill they once rode
O'er the green they all strode
Proud in their new green garb

Past church and pub
A desire for school grub
A welcome waiting inside

The school bell tolled
Their litter they hold
A sin to drop it about

Assembly was sombre
The band played longer
Two boys doth visit the gym

Tis break time once more
Kids queue at the door
Ten minutes of bliss breaks study

There's a rustle of paper
Boys scheme a quick caper
HM's approach spells danger

Girls knees once no show
With dress all too low
Mini skirts a boy's new delight

Come the end of the day
You bet none will stay
As school becomes quiet once more

CONTENTS

Rickmansworth School – Fifty Golden Years

		Page
	Acknowledgements	vii
	Appreciation for Illustrations	ix
	Foreword by Patricia, Countess Mountbatten of Burma	1
	Foreword by Dr Stephen Burton MA PhD	3
	Preface	5
	Local Maps	7
1	Rickmansworth	9
2	Scots Hill	11
3	Education Development – Locally and Nationally	15
4	The School Buildings – Conception to Completion	19
5	Clarendon School	23
6	Education – The Rickmansworth Way	27
7	The Management	31
8	A Headmaster's Overview	37
9	The House System	41
10	The School Status – Four Changes in Fifty Years	43
11	Six Decades of National History -- The Frugal Fifties	47
	The Swinging Sixties	48
	The Stormy Seventies	49
	The Affluent Eighties	50
	The Nervous Nineties	51
	And now – the Age of Reform	52
12	Fifty Years of Action	55
13	The Founding Fifties – The Decade of Firsts	57
14	The Sixties – Changes Loom Ahead	63
15	The Seventies – Reforms Now Bite Deep	67
16	The Eighties – Settled Times then More Change	71
17	The Nineties – Radical Restructuring Dominates	77
18	The New Century, the New Millennium – A Settled Future to Come?	83
19	Drama and Music	89
20	Sport – The Fifties	99
	The Sixties	103
	The Seventies	106
	The Eighties	107
	The Nineties	108
	And – Year 2000 Plus	110
21	Travel, Expeditions and Adventure	115
22	The Staff Room	123
23	Pupil Reflections	131
24	The Parents' Guild	143
25	The Old Students' Association – The Rosarians	145
26	In-house Publications	149
27	School Rules – 'Thou Shalt Not….'	153
28	School Statistics	155
	Epilogue	157

ACKNOWLEDGEMENTS

My thanks go to:-

Patricia, Countess Mountbatten of Burma CBE, CD, JP, DL

Mr Hugh Forsyth, Former Headmaster

Dr Stephen Burton, Current Headmaster

Mr Stephen Morrill, for access to Peter Morrill's archives

Mr Richard Gallimore, for family recollections of Millie Collings

Mr Dick Chapman, for editorial support

The Watford Observer

The Rickmansworth School Guild

The Rosarians Committee

Jane Morton, for continual support

Elizabeth Bowcock, for manuscript typing from my awful handwriting

All contributing teachers and pupils

And all those, too numerous to mention,
who have donated to this book

APPRECIATION FOR ILLUSTRATIONS

My thanks to the following who have kindly agreed to the publication of their contribution to the assortment of illustrations contained therein:

Alan Russell (Bury Lake Young Mariners)

Stephen Morrill

Dick Chapman

Tony Midson

Richard Taylor

Barry Kenyon

Gwyn Arch

Helen Franks (née Young)

Linda Baker (née Tansley)

Janice Field (née Watton)

Maureen Baldwin (née Camp)

Richard Gallimore

Hertfordshire County Council
Archives and Local Studies Department

Rickmansworth School Archives

The Watford Observer

For the cover picture – 'From the archive of the late Dr Ken Smith and Bury Lake Young Mariners Sailing Club, Rickmansworth Aquadrome'

My apologies to all former teachers and pupils for not including any class pictures – to do so would have meant the addition of some 500 photographs, a much fatter book, plus the chance that I would miss someone and 'sure as eggs are eggs' endure their wrath!

FOREWORD

by Patricia, Countess Mountbatten of Burma CBE, CD, JP, DL

I was very pleased to hear that Rickmansworth School has celebrated its Golden Jubilee, being the fifth new Grammar School to be built in the country after the war. It was started in September 1953 when seventy-five pupils formed the founding intake. They in turn were joined by a second intake of one hundred and thirty five pupils when the buildings were ready for occupation in 1954, before the school was officially opened in June 1956.

My mother, Edwina, Countess Mountbatten of Burma, was asked to perform the ceremony on that great day, with many activities marking such an exciting occasion. She was very pleased to be part of a day that marked the great steps forward that were being taken for the education of the first mainly post-war generation.

My mother knew how important this was because of her many and varied interests, which included the well-being and future of the nation's children. She had worked very hard all through the war for St John's Ambulance and rose to be Superintendent in Chief of the Women. She spent most of the terrible "blitz" air raid nights on London helping people in the East End shelters. Later she worked for our returning prisoners of war, particularly those from the Far East (where my father was Supreme Allied Commander) who had suffered so dreadfully.

I know how very pleased my mother was to see how the school was already establishing itself as a very important part of the community. It gives me pleasure too to have been asked to contribute a small piece to this book that marks the first fifty years of this flourishing school.

Patricia Mountbatten of Burma

Rt Hon. The Countess Mountbatten of Burma CI, GBE, DCVO
at the time of the opening of the school in 1956

FOREWORD

by Dr Stephen Burton MA PhD

Dr Stephen Burton

21st Century Rickmansworth School

It was BF Skinner (1904-90) who wrote that '*Education is what survives when what has been learned has been forgotten*'. I am sure that this book will revive memories of a remarkable education for all the Rosarians and school staff who glance through its pages. When I was appointed to succeed Hugh Forsyth as the third Headmaster in September 2000, I was aware that I was joining a good school with many excellent features. At Rickmansworth we continue to focus on individual potential by ensuring that all that we do as a school, for our pupils and staff and beyond into the wider community, is the very best we can strive for.

For all of you who have not forgotten the school, retain memories of the original buildings and have visited recently you will have realised that the core of Rickmansworth School has changed little from the early years.

However it didn't take long to realise that the School, which had benefited from 26 years of unbroken leadership, was in urgent need of investment. The Hertfordshire industrial 'design and build system' which was used in a massive school expansion programme in the 1950's and 1960's had an estimated 'life' of 60 years and much of Rickmansworth's infrastructure was in need of repair.

A Rickmansworth School Foundation, established with foresight by Hugh Forsyth and the Governing body, was ready to start a process of fund raising to improve the school. The school itself was now a Foundation School since the abolition of grant maintained status in 1999. The ten years of GM status had brought many things to the school in the 1990's but times had changed and the 'new' political focus was on school collaboration and partnership with the LEA. Bridges were built in the early years of the new millennium and whilst the school retains its independence we work closely with a number of organisations to access important services and funding.

The School has continued to grow in size with pupil numbers exceeding 1200 and teaching and support staff numbers growing to 120. Despite this growth the school still has a 'traditional' feel with an emphasis on those values laid down in the founding years: respect for the uniqueness of the individual and individual responsibility for maximising potential. Girls and boys still proudly wear the same school blazer worn by pupils decades ago. It was amazing to see 'old boys' with ties, blazers and colours, turn out for the Golden Jubilee Rugby Match on 13th March 2003. I was privileged to be invited to play in this game for the Rosarian XV, which also featured Chris Morton in the second row.

Several foundations were laid, which will guide the school during the first decade of the 21st century. In September the school's rich extra-curricular and curricular provision in the Arts was recognised by the DfES and the school awarded Arts College status. The 'creativity' at work in the school in the past and to some extent marginalised by government initiatives is now free to flourish. Investment in a new purpose built eight-classroom block and a substantial refurbishment programme in Science will help with the modernisation programme. In 2005 the school's plans to lead a Schools Sports Partnership were approved by the DfES and in the next three years the school will manage the growth of P.E. and sport in 46 primary and secondary schools. Next are plans for a new Sports Hall and Astroturf. The latter schemes all require substantial fundraising and the Foundation is active in raising funds from parents. Any Rosarians who feel able to contribute are actively encouraged to become involved and, in so doing, they will help to shape the next 50 years of a Rickmansworth School education.

PREFACE

It is my sincere recommendation that you don't treat this book as a novel by reading it from page one onwards, chapter by chapter. Pick and choose your route through as you wish, some chapters may be more relevant to you than others. The reason you ask – because it as a COFFEE TABLE BOOK to be 'dipped into' and read at will. Each chapter is self-standing, some follow on automatically, others are totally independent. What I hope to have achieved is an 'easy-read' chronicle of as many facts that I could uncover, from everything connected with the history of the area, the school, events and achievements and the 'icing' is personal reflections through anecdotes by both teachers and pupils. To include everyone's views – if I had ever been able to obtain them – would have resulted in a monstrously sized book that would probably have broken that coffee table in half! Luckily there is enough described within these covers to emphasise and confirm the spirit of camaraderie that Rickmansworth Grammar School always portrayed. (Sorry – it will always be grammar to me!).

'Nisi dominus aedifacaverit' – from Psalm 127 – *'except the Lord build this house, they labour in vain that build it'*. The Rickmansworth Urban District Council, whose support for a new school was overwhelming, gave their permission for this, their motto together with the coat of arms, to be officially adopted by the new Rickmansworth Grammar School as their badge. The full school crest includes the addition of the supporting dragons from the Clarendon School Badge.

No historical record of the times we enjoyed at Rickmansworth Grammar School, certainly for those of us as the founding intake of 1953, and our friends from the second intake who joined us at Scots Hills in 1954, and I hope every intake since then, can ever document every single event or occurrence at the school over the last fifty years.

This book follows on from my first one – 'The Founding Fifties, A Book of Firsts' – written to commemorate the ROSARIANS GOLDEN JUBILEE celebrations in July 2003 – highlighted the fact that in the fifties much of what we did and achieved, as the early intakes, was a FIRST, it was the first time in most cases that the occurrence or event had happened or been performed at the school. Such events were to lay down the benchmarks and set the standards for the future of the school – and that is what they precisely did. They are in many cases the foundation on which the school has been built and thereafter survived through some tumultuous times of change. A short extract from my first book will show you, the readers, how it all began.

> *In the fifties we were in an era of "in-between-ness", memories of World War Two were still very strong in our parents' minds, but not particularly in ours; most of us were only three years old when it ended. The fifties were a time of change – pleasant in between years before the era of the sixties came – themselves a time of radical, social and political change.*
>
> *It may be the Elstree Studios fictional interpretation of school kids from that era, boys dressed in short trous', long socks, shirt, tie and caps, with girls in skirts down below knee level, socks but no stockings, blouse and tie, hats, no make-up, and both with blazers sporting a regulation school badge, but its true – that's how we were. More than that, jewellery was forbidden (and for boys it had never been heard of), and there were no fluorescent designer bags for your 'bits and bobs', good old leather satchels with leather shoulder straps and polished brass buckles were the order of the day. Text books were issued on signature, not bought and owned as nowadays, many displaying after many years use a preponderance of*

> unruly remarks, with an early morning trip to the gym, if you were actually caught inscribing them with 1950's style graffiti. School lunches – one shilling for a full week – consisted of meat, two veg and over boiled gravy followed by pudding and lumpy custard. Those of us from Croxley were relieved of this daily ordeal; it was believed our health would be better served by a fitness session cycling home for lunch! Discipline was strict, you did as you were told, like it or not! Some didn't – and escaped – others less lucky paid the penalty. At least you knew where you stood in the fifties, and that wasn't only at school, my grandfather even made me empty my pockets at home every morning before I left. Mind you he was an ex Metropolitan Policeman. I didn't argue!

The school has celebrated 50 years by achieving high standards and results particularly in Education, Sport, Drama, Music and Art as a result of stable leadership. It was a school born out of the effects of a disastrous and hard fought World War, which if it had never happened, then the site at the top of Scots Hill may well have become a housing estate, a factory, or even remained as it was then, a peaceful stretch of woodland for people to ramble through.

I have examined some of the local history of the area, the effects of radical changes in education systems, how and why the buildings were constructed as they were, how the school was managed, how the effects of social, environmental and political changes over the second half of the last century had a bearing on the school, and how – because it gave so much opportunity to us – it was, and still is, a great school.

Though I personally left in 1960, along with many fond memories of my seven years there, I was not to return, or even make contact with any of my school chums for another 40 years, when in the year 2000 a chance visit to Rickmansworth gave me the opportunity to visit, meet with Hugh Forsyth the then Headmaster, be cajoled into joining the Rosarians, and 'hey presto', with the support of both Hugh and the current head, Dr. Stephen Burton, gradually become involved in recounting the history of the school. A little prompt in producing this book had come a couple or so years earlier when I had returned from a spell in South Africa in the early nineties. I began to unearth some of my old school press cuttings and dust covered relics and realised that I could not leave them to decay any longer. It was time to record in writing those special years I had enjoyed at school. Hence my first book – and now this, the full fifty golden years history of Rickmansworth Grammar School. My only confession – it will always be 'grammar' to me, as it will for a few others I suspect.

May I apologise in advance for any errors, omissions or incorrect facts that you may pick up, this book is compiled for 'coffee table' reading and is based on as much history as I have been able to uncover, and to this end I have acknowledged those who have so contributed. It can be used for reference, but in the end I could only reflect on what I have been able to uncover, and can of course remember!

Finally many thanks to all who have contributed, both in writing, on the telephone, or even in that strange modern way called e-mailing, a phenomenon that we had never even dreamt of in the fifties. Though the pace of life in this electronic age has increased enormously, we still carry out exactly the same activities as we did all those years ago – eating, sleeping, working, relaxing, talking, playing, writing, travelling, befriending and so on – the only difference is in those days it was at a leisurely pace – now it is breakneck speed. Whatever, we still end up doing and achieving exactly the same now as we did then.

And so what of the next fifty years, will they be as GOLDEN as the first fifty? Please read on and make your own judgment – but whilst doing so I hope you enjoy your read

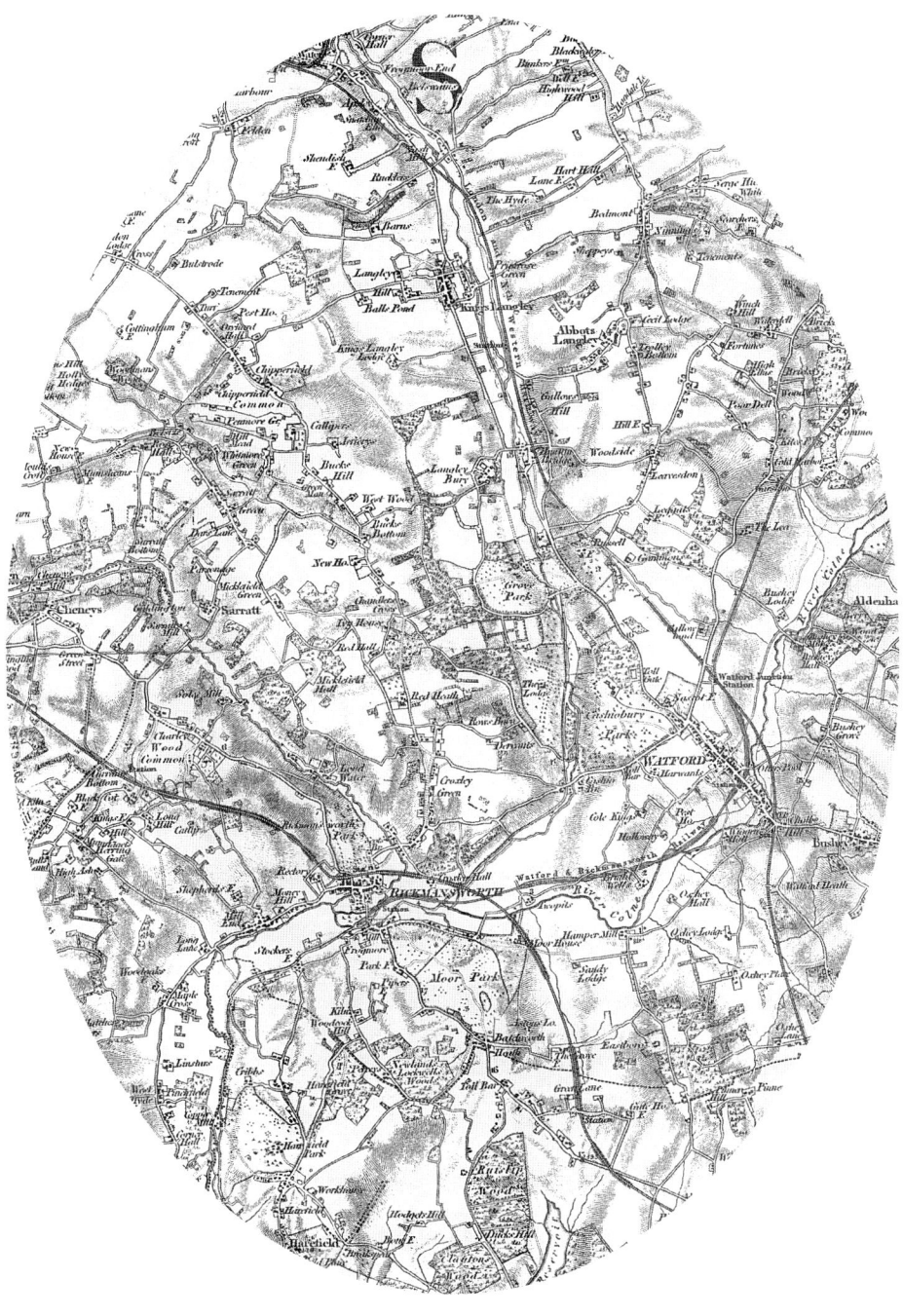

This map, of unknown origin, was printed around the year 1820, the railway lines as illustrated were added to it about seventy years later

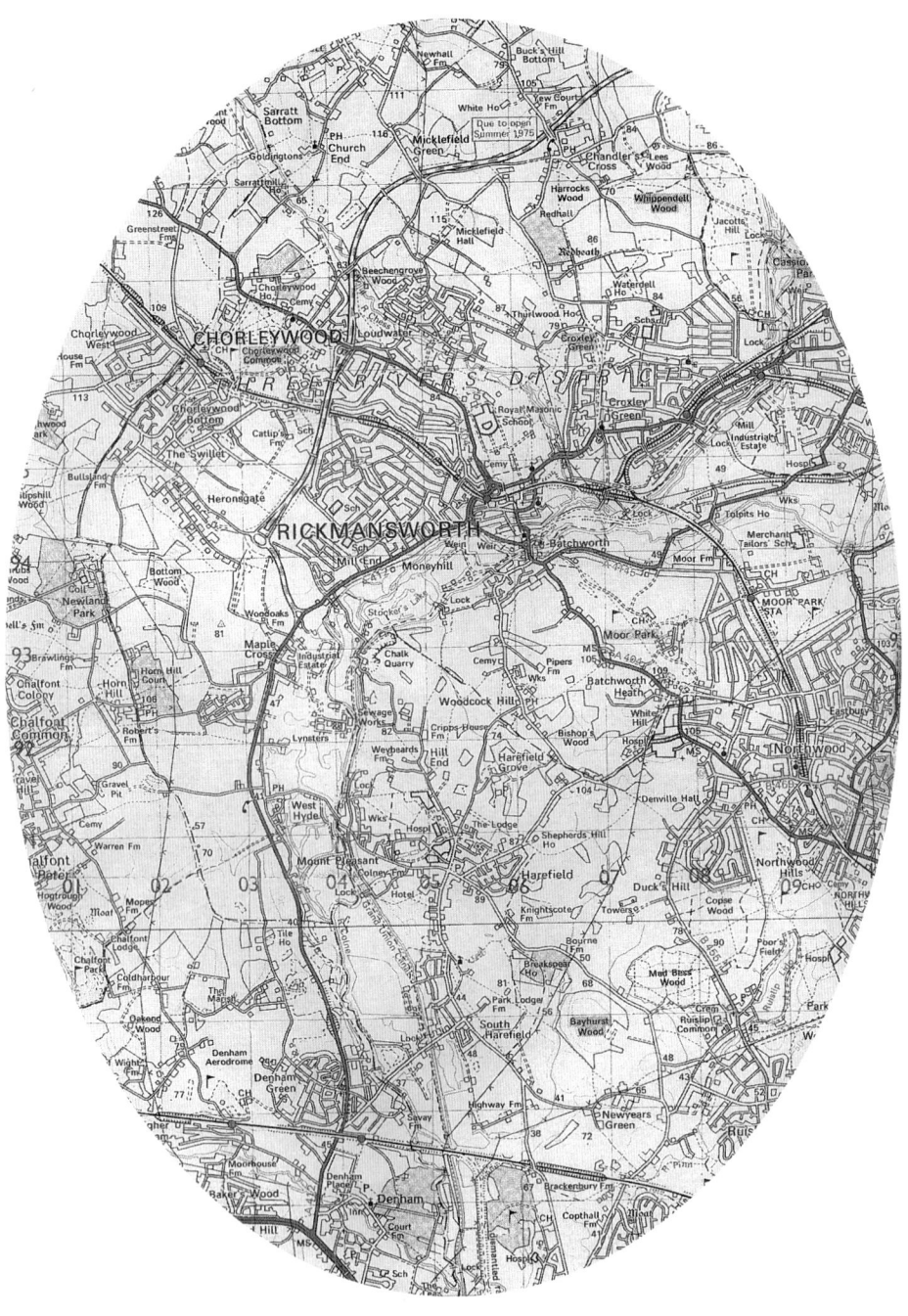

Modern day Rickmansworth and District

1

RICKMANSWORTH

Story has it that Rickmansworth, listed as 'The Manor of Prichemaresworde' and as described below in an extract from the eleventh century Doomsday Book, may have derived its name from a local landowner of the time, Mr Rykmer, Mr Rickman, or Mr Rick, a local man, the 'worth' coming from the Saxon word meaning 'farm or fenced land' having been added to his name. Croxley Green doesn't get a mention at all, itself only developing out of extensive tracts of farmland a century later, and then known as 'Crokesleya' or 'Croc's Lea', the field of 'Croc the Saxon'.

The small settlement, as can be seen, lay under the liberty of St. Albans, itself founded on the site of the Roman City of Verulamium, the place where the Magna Carta was actually drafted before being put to King John in the year 1214 at Runnymede.

> IN ST. ALBANS HUNDRED
>
> *The abbot himself holds RICKMANSWORTH. It is assessed at 15 hides. There is land for 20 ploughs, In demesne (are) 5 hides, and there are 3 ploughs, and there can be 2 more. There 4 Frenchmen and 22 villans with 9 bordars have 14 ploughs, and there can be 1 more. There are 5 cottars and 5 slaves, and 1 mill rendered 5s4d. meadow for 4 ploughs. From fish 4s pasture for the livestock. (and) woodland for 1,200 pigs. St. Alban held and holds this manor in demesne.*

Rickmansworth, or Ricky as it became affectionately known, remained a sleepy urban settlement for centuries. A market town without any famous battle honours – even from the wars that pitted Britain against France and Scotland during mediaeval age's right up to the Civil war of the sixteen hundreds. Only one notable warrior appeared when it was rumoured that Oliver Cromwell had taken refuge during that time in the Great Tithe Barn at Croxley Hall Farm, built in 1420, and a part of the Gonville and Caius landholding of the Manor of Croxley. The barn is one of the oldest and largest remaining in the UK, having been originally built for the Abbot of St. Albans. Much of the original internal timber remains and of course it is located only a stone's throw from the school playing fields in Croxley Hall Woods.

As years rolled on Rickmansworth had become a well known 'watering hole', when in 1756 the War Office called for a return on the number of inn beds available for billeting troops and rooms capable of stabling horses prior to the onset of the Seven Years War, started between Britain and her ally Prussia against France – yet again – but this time over competition for colonies.

In those records the Bell, Swan and George Inns in the High Street, and the Artichoke on Croxley Green all featured. By 1870 one wonders what the local working habits were as it seemed many were 'thirsty occupations' with Ricky boasting 32 inns, Croxley 4 and Chorleywood 13. In Croxley lay the George and Dragon, at the top of Scots Hill, the Artichoke, and Coach and Horses on the Green and the Gladstone Arms, a few hundred yards from the site of the new school, later renamed the Duke of York when neighbouring Garden Road was changed to Yorke Road in honour of the Chairmen of the Urban District Councils. (Recounting this does not confirm the truth that as a rugby player I have visited them all!).

Closing on modern times, in 1887 the first train on the extended Metropolitan Railway line arrived to what was described by one of the three passengers on that first day as a "one eyed place with a straggling street in which there were half a dozen weather beaten public houses, a number of small cottages, a couple of butchers' shops and a mineral water manufacturers establishment". This probably referred to Franklins and not Springwells, themselves located further away in Mill End. The latter however did become famous for their alliance with Moussec, who by 1932 had acquired the Brewery Malting site, close to St. Joan of Arc's Convent School and opposite the Picture House Cinema. Moussec, a champagne perry drink, 'mousse' the French for sparkling, 'sec' the French for dry, was first sold by Springwells to public houses at 1/3d a bottle. Moussec products still exist, Springwells folded years ago.

The Picture House Cinema or 'Bug Hutch' as it was more often known, became famous, not for the variety of films shown, but because it created, in meteorological terms, one of the best 'frost hollows' known in the world. The phenomenon was caused by its sighting in a valley, close to a river and where the railway embankment ran through the valley. The actual frost hollow was to be found along the footpath between the cinema and embankment, and on a cold winter's night temperatures could be recorded between six to ten degrees below the surrounding air temperature. Its cause – the cold air had rolled off the gentle valley slopes, crossed the chill of the river and had been trapped in the 'hollow'. A meteorological handbook could probably describe the phenomenon better!

And so Rickmansworth had survived the good and the bad of a thousand years, had emerged reasonably unscathed after the World War and was by the nineteen fifties a thriving town nestling in the green belt, on the fringe of London. And so in 1953 another landmark was created on the fringe of the town with the erection of its own grammar school, a school big enough to rival neighbouring Watford Boys and Girls Grammar and situated at the top of Scots Hill.

The school's emergence was to change the face of Rickmansworth and Croxley Green forever!

Sleepy Ricky – in the fifties

2

SCOTS HILL

Scots Hill, classified as trunk route number A412 and famed for its bends and steepness, lies between Rickmansworth and Watford. Until 1972, when it became a dual carriageway, the hill was a simple two-lane highway – one up – one down. At the bottom a sharpish right hand bend takes the road over the Chess River Bridge and around the prominent and enclosed Scotsbridge House, home since 1953 to the British Friesian Society (now Holstein UK), before bearing left past Copthorne Road and into a virtually unsighted, sudden and ever increasing steep uphill slope, before levelling out at the top.

The Hill

These two bends and the uphill slope caused continual havoc with the less sophisticated gearboxes of motor vehicles during the first three quarters of the twentieth century. Many a time a bus would come to an abrupt halt halfway up the slope, unable to cope, and with no alternative but to disgorge all of its passengers, many of them schoolchildren, to "lighten the load". It would then creep in low gear to the top to catch up these forlorn souls who had managed to walk up quicker.

Heavily laden tankers fared even worse. After causing widespread congestion as they failed to overcome the steep slope they were forced to retreat slowly downhill to seek an alternative route; those who chose Copthorne Road for this option were more than likely to incur the wrath of many a disgruntled resident – it was after all a private road!

Through the late eighteen hundreds, and up to the early nineteen fifties, the half a mile of road running from the top of the hill to the junction with the Green, itself marked by the prominent spire of All Saints Parish Church, formed a "village within a village". This section of Scots Hill, within the boundaries of Croxley Green, housed a thriving, though small, community.

The road was lined either side by rows of cottages, two public houses, a gospel hall, four shops, a prominent windmill, still milling corn at the turn of the twentieth century, and of course dominated by All Saints Church.

In front of the church stood the Berean Cottages, designed as Alms Houses and built in 1837. They were affectionately known as "Penny Row", based on the original weekly rent paid by the elderly inhabitants. After the Great War they were renamed 'Heroes Row' when they were inhabited by returning ex servicemen, the rent having increased 36 fold to a massive 3/- per week. The cottages were eventually demolished in 1932 and replaced by a new church hall.

The top of Scots Hill, the Gospel Hall and Penny Row a century ago

The Second World War took its toll on this little Scots Hill community, the church, church hall and one pub, the Sportsman, were all damaged by bombs in 1941, and again in 1944. On the 19th February 1943 the Gospel Hall and its adjoining cottages were destroyed by an infamous flying bomb – a doodlebug – and the land laid dormant, until eventually in 1954 becoming the site around the entrance to the new grammar school.

In the fifties some of the cottages close to the hill, together with the George and Dragon Pub and two shops, were demolished by contractors in order to make way for new housing. Some buildings however remained, including Luxtons the newsagent, formerly W F Eager until the outbreak of the war, the adjacent and former grocers shop once owned by Benjamin H. Ward, the Sportsman's pub, the windmill (now a house) and the church, all of which have survived to this day.

Croxley Hall Woods, before the school was even a dream

2 – Scots Hill

With planning for the new grammar school starting in 1950, its opening in 1954 was to transform the peace and tranquillity of sleepy Scots Hill forever. Early in 2004, Luxtons the newsagents, for fifty years the early morning and late afternoon port of call for so many of the 8,000 or more pupils who attended the school, closed its doors for the very last time, maybe one landmark at the top of Scots Hill has gone forever, but the biggest of them all will go on – and on!

Evidence!

3

EDUCATION DEVELOPMENT – LOCALLY AND NATIONALLY

"The debauchery of profanity amongst the poor sort, brought about by a great ignorance of religion amongst them" – said the Rev. John James in 1711, then vicar in the Parish of Rickmansworth as he described the widespread illiteracy that prevailed in those days.

His remedy – a school; to fund it – a charity, the result – donations from the local gentry totalling in all £15, 'thousands' in today's values. From this he had enough to found a school and pay the first quarter's bills, a far cry from the awesome demands of modern day budgeting! Where the school was located and what its name was has faded in the mists of time. It did however provide a base for teaching those impoverished waifs – through the eyes of Rev. James – in the art of reading, writing and the ways of the Christian Religion. His very vision had laid the foundations for modern schooling in the neighbourhood.

Up until the twentieth century education of the masses in the country did not feature highly on the agenda, though attempts to improve standards continued, albeit against a backdrop of poverty. In 1836 the Rickmansworth Poor House had been converted into a school, with segregated girls and boys classes and it continued in use until closure in 1936.

If your family were affluent they paid for you to be educated, if not your schooling ended very early in life, if perhaps you even went to school. Life for the uneducated was one destined for the mines, workhouses or on the land. Reading and writing wasn't necessary for these 'careers'!

By the onset of the twentieth century changes were rapidly evolving, the neighbourhood of Rickmansworth by then housed three "affluent" schools – St. Joan of Arc's Convent for Girls, opened with only nine founding pupils and in the building once the home of the nineteenth century novelist George Eliot, Merchant Taylor's Boys School and the Royal Masonic Girls School – relocated from London in 1934. Grammar School education was available for both sexes, but only in nearby Watford.

The biggest influence on education however came about with the advent of the Second World War, and the repercussions it brought about on society.

Between 1941 and 1943 there had been a marked increase in the national birth rate, no explanation was required, the "War Bulge Babies" had arrived. By 1944, with the world war turning in the favour of the allies, a new government body was founded – the Ministry of Education. As the war ended in 1945 it was back to domestic business, rebuilding and recovering after the ravages of war. This in turn led to the introduction of new structures in the country. The Labour Party had won the post war election and was determined to reform working and social practises.

Their first and far-reaching Act of Parliament in 1944 was to have a major impact on schooling over the succeeding fifteen years. It provided for segregation of public education into primary and secondary stages, introduction of the eleven plus, an end to fee-paying in maintained schools, and 'county colleges' to be able to support education to the age of eighteen. In other words, a tripartite system of grammar, technical and secondary modern schools had been created overnight! The school leaving age was raised to fifteen, the first such change since it was initially set at fourteen in 1918. By 1951 the old Higher School and

School Certificates were replaced by the General Certificate of Education – GCE "O" and "A" levels were born – to be taken mainly in grammar schools.

South West Hertfordshire, now with its own Local Education Authority (LEA), had by the early fifties felt the dramatic effects of the population boom where from a war-time figure of 25,000 eligible for all schooling ages, by 1950 had seen this figure rise to 56,000. This, added to the rise in school leaving age, meant that an urgent and radical overhaul of the whole education system was required to cope with the increased numbers.

By-laws were also being passed nationally to close the loophole whereby unscrupulous employers could employ school age children. Fifteen was the lowest legal age, no longer could little twelve year-old Johnny skip school, play truant and earn the princely sum of 1/-, enough for 48 'black jacks'!

As a result of all these changes the need for new local secondary schools in the area was imperative. Two new secondary modern schools were opened; the first, William Penn in Mill End, named after this well known local dignitary of the eighteenth century who was granted land in North America by King Charles the first, calling it Pennsylvania; and the second, Durrants School, erected on the former farm estate of the same name that occupied what is now much of Croxley Green.

With the desperate need also having arisen for an additional local grammar school to relieve both Watford and Bushey Grammars, Rickmansworth was founded, to become the fifth new one to be built in the country since the war, destined for opening in 1953, and to be located on reclaimed woodland at the top of Scots Hill, Croxley Green. Fifty years on it still remains, while William Penn and Durrants have long since been closed and demolished, despite attempts by the authorities to amalgamate all three as one school many years later.

*Educational aids –
'then and now'*

3 – Education Development – Locally and Nationally

On the national front the future concept of comprehensive schooling was born in 1954 with the opening of the first of its kind – Kidbrooke School in South London – heralding over the next two decades an ever-increasing number of such schools.

Nationally it was decided that cycling to school would require the passing of a police sponsored Cycling Proficiency Test. Added to this Police Bicycle Inspectors school visits became normal, a failed test, a wonky pedal or more dastardly no brakes, cable cut by a spurned boy/girl friend, would mean walking to school – a hazardous exercise, particularly on the upward section of Scots Hill in a December snowstorm!

By 1955 unrest was building nationally over the inequality between male and female teachers' salaries. The problem was addressed by the Burnham Committee, who saw fit to introduce equal pay for both, but for it to be phased in over a series of stages. Maybe a prelude to equal rights and opportunities?

More progress was felt by 1959 when the Ministry of Education proposed a programme designed to ensure that by 1980 at least half of all full-time pupils would remain in education until they were eighteen.

All this progress spelt good news, on another front by the end of the fifties changing facilities had improved with hot water now available and earth toilet closets had been replaced in all schools, the mind boggles (or 'bog (gles)') at what school life used to be like!

In the sixties development was rapid, open universities became reality, and in 1964 planning started on the new comprehensive schooling concept, designed to cater for 'pupils of all abilities', as it expanded rapidly as a combined replacement for grammar and secondary modern schooling. A year later the new Department of Education and Science, which replaced the old 'Ministry', introduced the new Certificate of Secondary Education (CSE) as an alternative to 'O' levels and to be taken mainly in secondary modern schools.

The seventies saw many changes, free school milk was abolished in 1971, school-leaving age was raised to sixteen in 1972 and the Education Act compelling the introduction of comprehensive schools was introduced in 1976, only to be repealed in 1979!

That old favourite, corporal punishment, was abolished in inner London schools in 1976, and nationwide by 1986. The threat of 'six of the best' for propelling an ink soaked pellet of blotting paper at the back of your most unfavourite of teacher's head while they scribed at the blackboard, was reduced to "one hundred lines – I mustn't do it again sir".

The next twenty years up to the turn of the century saw many more changes – some major, some minor, some introduced successfully, others later scrapped. Assisted places were introduced in independent schools, but abolished in 1997, a technical and vocational initiation was introduced for the mid teens, and O' Levels and 'CSE's' were abolished in favour of a new General Certificate of Education (GCSE) in 1986, the same year as National Vocational Qualifications (NVQ's) were introduced.

The National Curriculum, aimed at giving core subjects that are compulsory to the age of sixteen, and Grant Maintained status were introduced in 1988 through the Education Reform Act of that year, deemed the "biggest" since 1947, only for the latter to be replaced by Foundation status ten years later.

GNVQ's (General National Vocational Qualifications offered as a less academic alternative to 'A' level), SAT's (Standard Attainment Tests for seven, eleven and fourteen year olds), AS

(Advanced Supplementary Qualification) all became common place by the mid-nineties. The age of abbreviations!

By 1992 Polytechnics were granted full university status after yet another Act of Parliament thus relieving LEA's (Local Education Authorities) of control of sixth form colleges and not to be forgotten, primary education received a boost with the introduction in 1997 of a National Literacy Strategy. The three 'R's' reared their ugly head again!

By 2000 the Advanced Subsidiary (AS Level) exams were introduced, replacing the old AS qualification and taken half way through the two year 'A' level course. This time a pass provided a qualification in its own right.

And so the decade, century and millennium all ended with education in the country having undergone a massive uplift since World War Two at a pace that surpassed anything ever tried or dreamt of in the previous two hundred years. Rickmansworth survived the turmoil of no less than four changes in its status, where many another school folded under such strain.

There are no doubts that the standards and quantity of education now available outstrips what was available when the school opened in 1953, but in the end the finished product is the same – an educated young person ready and able to be let loose in the big wide world, with much more available to them, but probably no better a 'beast' than those similarly turned out at the outset of Rickmansworth Grammar School in the fifties.

4

THE SCHOOL BUILDINGS – CONCEPTION TO COMPLETION

It was not until 1945 that specific responsibility for the building of new schools in the county was vested in one single organisation – the Hertfordshire County Architects Department.

With plans laid down in the early fifties to build the new grammar school on sixteen acres of reclaimed woodland at the top of Scots Hill, local Architects Henry & Chitty were appointed to work alongside the county council with its design, Universal Housing Company being contracted to build the edifice. It was prescribed to accommodate a maximum of 630 pupils, plus associated staff and designed as four separate blocks, but later changed with three being joined up.

Originally budgeted at £188,000, which would suffice for a three bedroom terraced house in today's world, the eventual cost was a quarter of a million pounds and this may have seemed a lot in the fifties, but an analysis of the scale of the building work would show that it was a "no frills" construction, the basics only would suffice. It was after all a limited life construction designed to last only 60 years.

The availability of steel and some construction materials in those early post war years was strictly controlled and buildings designed wholly of a steel frame construction were quite rare. This factor dictated the original layout in four separate blocks, with the science block to be built around a steel reinforced concrete frame, the assembly hall block around load bearing brick walls with conventional welded steel roof trusses and the classroom and gymnasium blocks around the "8'3" grid" concept. Whilst steel reinforced, and load bearing brick style construction is maybe easy for the uninitiated to understand, without the need to explain in detail, the 8'3" concept is little known.

In the early Sixties

An engineer named Hinchcliffe, based at the West Bromwich construction firm of Hills, devised a steel frame of these dimensions in order to conform to a suggestion made in 1944 that schools should be planned around modules of that strange size. It was basically a 'prefabricated steel trestle box building kit', being finished off with the addition of concrete cladding slabs. Given an ideal world the materials and appearance of the system might have been different, but architects at the time did not live in such a world, building materials were scarce, and there were few options available, so the 8'3" system had few alternatives.

The reason for the decision to join three blocks is not plain, but the one to keep the gymnasium block more isolated was logical. It was far enough away to hide the noisy activities of the associated woodwork and metalcraft classrooms, the smells from the

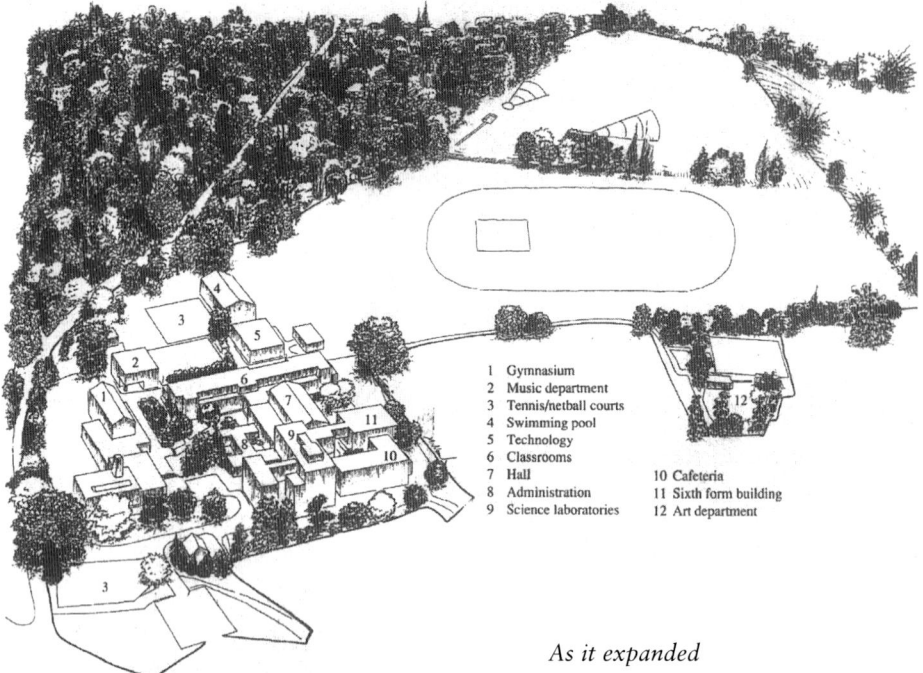

As it expanded

kitchen and the grunts and groans from the gymnasium and it also hid the noise of the delivery trucks and tankers proceeding to the co-located boiler house.

The overall 'finish' of the blocks was provided by the application of pre-cast concrete units to the floors and flat roofing, with the latter in the science block being of hollow construction. Ceilings were generally of fireproofed wall board, suspended on aluminium tees allowing room for 'service' pipes in between.

The assembly hall and gymnasium floors were both of solid wood, with the hall prepared in a solid parquet style at a cost of £3,000, a fact that pupils were constantly reminded of in those early years. Walking on it was a tricky business – if the headmaster was around!

The original design allowed for the school to be set back far enough to give room for the two lane road to be widened and full sized roundabout to be constructed, with the extra space becoming available through planned demolition of the remaining row of cottages. To this day the road remains the same, only a mini roundabout has appeared and the cottages still stand!

Opened a year behind schedule in 1954, in 50 years the site has expanded to 26 acres, the original buildings remain very much as they were in external appearance, but with much improvement internally. Many new blocks have been added since the sixties, they were needed to cope with the rise in pupil population from the original 630 to a figure just over 1,100 – close to a 100% rise.

The original concept of a limited life building can however still be seen albeit only occasionally, as the rapid deterioration that was so apparent in the fifties has now largely been rectified. No doubt the school and its original buildings will see in the centennial celebrations in style – in 2053.

4 – The School Buildings – Conception to Completion

Before too many extra buildings

A pupils' appraisal of the school buildings and surrounds, written in the early sixties, sums up just how unforeseen was the rapid expansion of the school and how inadequate the buildings were.

> *See it first between half past eight and nine on a weekday morning with the pupils, teeming in, will show you how it is used.*
>
> *The approach is what one might expect from a post-war grammar school one hundred yards of grass and then a white paling fence which combine to give a pleasantly spacious and rural tone. The drive divides this grass and one enters through white gates to be faced with an oval of more grass. The impression of spacious living is marred when the drive becomes a seething mass of pupils and staff cars. Unfortunately, this trend to overcrowding is one also to be found in the school buildings.*
>
> *These are now before you. The angularity of their post-war style, which employs a great deal of glass, and concrete, has been nicknamed "Druid's Rococo": by one Sunday paper. The other principal materials are red brick and yellow rough-cast concrete which in winter seem to draw up the cold and wet into themselves: in summer, the concrete at least is pure sun-baked Mexicana. The business-like red brick and concrete contrast effectively with the surrounding woods, and the beautiful Chess and Colne valleys.*
>
> *Inside, however, the décor has been less well thought out. Many of the floors are cold tile, and the walls form stark angles with the coldly functional steel-raftered ceilings. This institutional and uncomfortable style is at odds with the flowing*

wood floors around the hall and library, and with the paste-board partitions put up throughout the school to provide more rooms. Everywhere you can see the need for space – in the crammed desks and the sixth form's forlorn kettles for break-time coffee lying conspicuous in the midst of a Maths lesson.

It is a curious mixture, this school; angular, uncomfortable, yet set in woodland; expensively built but already inadequate, its basic attractiveness hidden by the piled satchels, the partitions and the jungles of furniture.

Lying in a suburb which still boasts a village green, Rickmansworth Grammar School is a mixture of town and country and has a mixture of pupils.

A footnote in local architect Andrew Saint's 1987 publication "Towards a Social Architecture – the role of school building in post war England" quotes:

"Scots Hill Grammar School, Rickmansworth (1952-4) by Robert Hening and the red-baiter, Anthony Chitty, was sometimes cited as an example of the mess that could be made of the 8 feet 3 inches system".

─────────── maybe so, but it is still standing as it will for many more years, so much for limited life construction!

Nearing completion, forty years on

CLARENDON SCHOOL

With the schedule for completion of the new Scots Hill site in 1953 having slipped a year, alternative accommodation was needed for those 75 pupils already awarded places at Rickmansworth Grammar School, but with nowhere to go.

Clarendon School, a new Secondary Modern Establishment in Oxhey, itself only having been completed and opened a couple of years, won the 'dubious recognition' of accommodating the homeless eleven year olds. There was stiff competition for this "honour", Hampden Secondary Modern, also in Oxhey, had been a serious contender too!

In September 1953 those pupils from Croxley Green and Rickmansworth were collected by coach on day one from the appointed pickup points and duly delivered, fresh faced, to Clarendon on their new adventure, not only to experience the transition from primary to secondary education, but also to become the founder pupils at the beginning of the new Rickmansworth Grammar School, albeit with a different start than may have been envisaged. Pupils from Watford, Bushey and Oxhey were less fortunate in their transport arrangements; they had to make their own way to Clarendon.

Children at that age usually take little time to make friends, and very soon most of the 75 pioneers had gelled well with each other.

Maroon Clarendon School uniforms were worn by all, but the 'upstairs/downstairs' system soon prevailed when the 'Grammar Grubs', as they were known, were both housed and taught in a separate block from the rest of Clarendon's incumbents. The only gelling factor between the two "schools" was that of the new Headmaster, fresh from the British Military School in Wilhelmshaven, West Germany – Peter Morrill, PJTM as often known by his staff

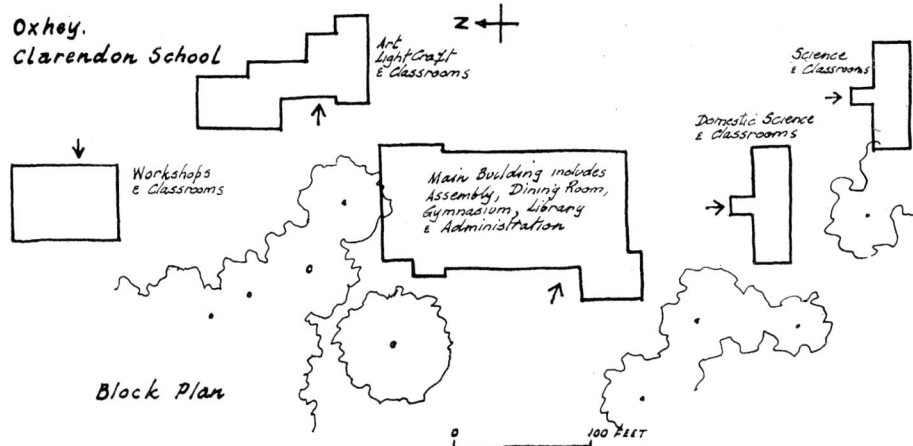

– was Headmaster of both schools. Eileen Flint, who lived locally in Oxhey claimed the right, quite correctly, to be classed as the first ever pupil to attend Rickmansworth Grammar School – though due to an administrative error. She had taken her eleven plus exams and interview in Harpenden, but when she moved back to Oxhey she had to go for another interview as it was a different catchment area. Just before the start of term, September 1953, a

The 'Grammar Grubs' block

message was passed to her parents that she had been allocated a place at the new Rickmansworth Grammar School that would operate from Clarendon School for the first year. An information pack containing all details was promised, but never arrived. As she lived only two minutes walk from Clarendon School she just went in on the first day of term. Her name was not called for any of the classes so she was escorted to the office for the situation to be resolved. She then found out that the grammar school classes did not start for another week! She was not allowed to go home that day; instead she was put to work with a 'number stamping device' in a room filled with books. The 'issue number' had

Typical lunchtime – to music no less!

to be stamped inside the front of each book. She did not complete the task and happily had the rest of the week off.

The next week, still with no further information about the new school, she arrived to join her classmates. Her delight rapidly turned to despair and chagrin when they all got off of the bus in the new Clarendon School uniforms. Living locally she knew that hardly any pupils wore school uniform (perhaps only the brass band/school teams), it was not compulsory. She was wearing a blue corduroy pinafore dress and white blouse! Obviously the next Saturday morning was spent in the uniform shop kitting her out to look like the rest of the 'grammar grubs'.

The morning coach trips, conducted by Vanguard Coaches from Garston, North Watford, chose suitable pick up points, each one conveniently outside a local newsagents and sweet shop. Pocket money for school rarely exceeded sixpence a day, more than enough for six one penny chews, or 24 'farthing' black jacks, purchased before boarding the coach. They become useful for break time bartering – particularly in exchange for stamps, as your author I know – I exchanged a penny chew for an '1840 twopenny blue stamp', I hope the vendor doesn't remember!

Normal subjects were taught, sports were played, though not representative, and at the end of the first and third (summer) terms pupils sat exams. Papers were marked, graded and form positions were given. That was the last time class grading ever happened in Rickmansworth Grammar School – it was abandoned as from 1954. Though this could have been a forerunner maybe to banning competitiveness amongst children on a national scale, thankfully in Rickmansworth Grammar School it was not, competitiveness remained dominant on the sports field, as strong from the start as it is today.

In July 1954 those 75 pioneers said goodbye to Clarendon School and after a well-deserved summer break prepared themselves for life at the new premises at Scots Hill.

6

EDUCATION – THE RICKMANSWORTH WAY

Once established at Scots Hill it became easier to lay down the ground rules – the three 'Rs – reading/writing/arithmetic' were of paramount importance. With only fourteen members of staff starting in 1954, including the headmaster and headmistress, the scope of the curriculum was very limited. Though broader than the three 'Rs it was much less than offered in modern day schooling. The basics were Maths, English (language and literature), History, Geography, Art, Religious Instruction, French, Physics, Chemistry, Biology and Physical Education (PE). Latin was available if one was so 'inclined', Domestic Science was available for the girls and Woodwork & Metalcraft for the boys.

By the end of the first decade the scope of subjects available had doubled, and after 50 years it is impossible to list. In that first year in 1954 at Scots Hill there were barely 230 pupils, by the turn of the century it had become almost 1,200, with around 65 teachers.

A mere calculation will show that the pupil to teacher rate has altered very little over the fifty years – still hovering at approximately sixteen to one.

Education methods, standards and scope have however changed radically from when the first sixth form came into being in 1958 when the choice was very limited – you either went to science – a combination of Physics, Chemistry, Biology and Maths, or to the Arts – English, History, Geography and Art. There were no in betweens, there was nothing else. A startling revelation at that time was the fact that only three teachers had ever taught to 'A' Level before that year. Their achievements were as equally commendable as those of the pupils when the first 'A' Levels were taken in 1960.

Marigold Hunter, who had gained the top overall mark of 98% in the whole of the UK in 'O' Level Geography, repeated her performance by gaining the highest marks nationally at Advanced-Scholarship Level Geography, Oxford & Cambridge Joint Board, and was awarded the Royal Geographical Society Prize, and a princely sum of five guineas! In 1963 John Carvey repeated the performance, only for Jane Hardy to do the same in 1964. No mean feat within four years especially against other 'contestants', including those from Eton, Harrow, Winchester and Watford Grammar! To add to this, and put the icing on the cake, Nicholas Wyndow gained distinctions in both A Level Maths and Physics in 1960. Any theory that these original teachers might have been daunted and unprepared for their thrust into sixth form teaching was dispelled by these achievements.

During the mid sixties the school was selected to pilot the Nuffield 'O' Level Physics project, which enjoyed a very practical bias to science teaching. The project was later extended to include 'A' Level as well. This was considered to be a very stimulating and challenging time for both staff and pupils and a 'new' part of the course was a two-week stretch devoted to a practical topic, starting from scratch and then to be written up as a scientific paper. An example of such topics includes two pupils taking on the problem of analysing the factors that affect the life of soap bubbles. Initially bubbles were timed at lasting only a few seconds – but at the end of the fortnight it was 24 hours. They achieved this by eliminating dust and water vapour from the atmosphere around the bubble – changing soap solution concentrations and eventually finding a resting place with virtually no vibrations. These were exciting, and some may say earth-shattering, times in the physics laboratories! What this actually proved to the art of washing up the soap dishes does not appear to have been recorded.

Andrew Western, as Head of Physics at the time, was closely involved with the London Planetarium designing a session suitable for GCSE Nuffield 'O' Level Physics. The director of the time, John Ebdon, acknowledged publicly the School's assistance and many years later invited Mr. Western to the Planetarium Silver Jubilee in recognition of his efforts.

By end of the Sixties, 1969 in fact, four – 'Oxbridge' Scholarships were achieved by pupils – the only school in Hertfordshire to achieve this feat.

During the seventies and eighties the average number of university places gained by pupils annually was 38, with an average annual intake of approximately 150 this equated to an average of 26%. Year 1977 was the best at 56 whilst 1987 slumped to only twenty pupils. During this time the percentage of 'O' Level pupils who passed the 'Oxbridge' combined Board English exam was recorded as amongst the highest in the country and the school regularly sent a number of second and third year pupils to the Royal Institution Master Class in Maths at Hatfield Polytechnic, in addition to taking part in County Schools Mathematics Quiz's.

Honours in education in the eighties and nineties include a host of girls winning the annual Ashdown County Scholarships, such names include Helen Gunn, Celine Matthews, Katherine Dustan, Tessa Brown, Rachael Tahens-Milne, Imogen Wilson, Helen Rudge, Sumanjit Gill and Caroline Adams, and by the end of the eighties two girls, Fiona Mackay and Christine Hulsay, had been awarded the Associated Examining Board Medal for obtaining the top grade in the UK in 'A' Level Biology.

And so at the end of the 'fifty golden years' every conceivable subject available is taught at Rickmansworth School. With traditions high in the sporting, drama and music fields, to name but a few, it is pleasing to the eye to see the school feature around the middle of the table for the top 100 academic achievers in the lists published regularly every year in the national newspapers. That is an achievement of distinction when considering the 'turmoil' caused by the four 'status' changes during those years and one that has not been experienced by many of the other schools on the lists. Stability helps – Rickmansworth has stability and has been a survivor.

As a lasting memory of two of the three Rs – reading and writing – here follows the basis devised in 1956 on the 'cultivation' of speaking, reading and writing English, followed by a list of books recommended as aids to achieve this during the first four years at school. See how many you can remember ever reading?

Scheme of work for English – August 1956

The Aim
> The aim is to cultivate the ability to speak, read and write English with intelligence, accuracy and enthusiasm.

Pronunciation
> The example of the staff is of prime importance. They should have, or adopt a universally acceptable pronunciation, and encourage pupils to do the same. In many cases practice in speech training will be necessary. All pupils should have frequent opportunity for reading aloud. Cases of mispronunciation should be corrected with tact, and at the discretion of the member of staff concerned. Pupils with definite speech defects can receive individual attention at the clinics, if the matter is reported to the school Doctor.

Poetry

> "And let us, ciphers of the great accompt,
> On your imaginary forces work". (Prologue Henry V)

Poetry is written to be enjoyed; it is not a difficult exercise, devised by odd people called poets. Enjoyment and appreciation of the verse are the first essentials. This appreciation depends largely on good reading. Often it is beneficial for the poem to be read first by the teacher, but opportunity should be given for all pupils to read aloud, either together, or individually, or if the poem is unsuitable for this treatment, entirely by the individual. Verse composition should be encouraged, not insisted upon. Passages to be learnt by heart may be set at reasonable intervals. These should be passages which appeal to the form as a whole, or may be a free choice on the part of the pupils.

Oral Composition

Oral Composition is essential in all forms. Suitable practices are the recapitulation of matter read, seen or heard; occasional discussions; the giving of directions to visitors, in the street, or round the school; explaining the difficulties and customs to foreigners, etc.

Reading

The ultimate aim is to reveal the mind of a great author at work. This realisation, which will come to some, if not all, should be developed in easy stages, through the appreciation of an easy tale, a story written with the purpose, a book written because the author had to write it.

In the younger forms, the most important part of any reading period is the understanding of what is read. Suitable practices are discussion of the story, stage by stage, of characters in the plot; and in more detail, selection of topic sentences. This may be linked with lessons on sentences and paragraph construction, and gives much opportunity for work study. As the course progresses, interruptions should be eliminated. Silent reading periods are often of more value than reading aloud individually.

Drama

> "Thou cans't not speak of that thou dost not feel". Romeo and Juliet.

The first essential is to suggest that what is being attempted is only a poor second-best to seeing the play on the stage. Ideally, the play should be seen, by as many pupils as possible. The play should come off the printed page, by a performance by the pupils, by a prepared acted-reading, or by the teacher keeping the stage in the forefront of the pupils' minds. This applies particularly to Shakespearean plays.

Some introduction concerning the Elizabethan theatre, and audience, is usually of great benefit. In the subsequent reading, the teacher should select for himself the part which will give most help in binding the whole together, and serve as a model for pupils' later reading.

Characters should always be discussed as living beings, and reference to what is in the text insisted upon.

Grammar

The teaching of grammar is essential, especially in the early stages, though it should be treated rather as the means to the end, than as the end itself. Whenever possible it should be related to the texts read. Co-ordination with the modern language and classical departments is desirable and often vital.

Written Composition

The ability to write clearly, attractively and correctly should be the aim in composition: the development of the art of putting ideas across to someone else in persuasive and palatable form. The practical aspect should always be stressed; letters, book reviews, magazine articles, diary entries, etc. Form magazines should be encouraged, but should be the children's work, not the teacher's. Quality is of more importance than quantity. If subject requiring imaginative treatment are set alternatives requiring clear and logical exposition should be given. The pitfalls of imaginative subjects should be borne in mind, and pupils warned of them as the course progresses.

Books recommended for reading – first to fourth years

Wright	A first dictionary
Ridout	English to-day – Books 1 to 4
Kenneth Graham	Wind in the Willows
Dickens	Christmas Carol
Spyri	Heidi
Kipling	Puck of Pook's Hill
Stevenson	Kidnapped/Black Arrow
H.G. Wells	First Man in the Moon
John Buchan	Prester John
Shakespeare	Twelfth Night/Merchant of Venice/Julius Caesar
Jack London	White Fang
Cervantes	Don Quixote
R.C. Sherriff	Badger's Green
Goldsmith	She Stoops to Conquer/ The Deserted Village
J.B. Priestley	Our Nation's Heritage
Polgrave	Golden Treasury
Blackmore	Lorna Doone
Goldsmith	Vicar of Wakefield
Hardy	Greenwood Tree/Far from the Madding Crowd
Shaw	Pygmalion

7
THE 'MANAGEMENT'

As with any establishment, if it is not managed and led effectively and strongly, success borders on zero, and closure looms. It is a tribute to the management structure of Rickmansworth School that it has passed successfully through periods of enormous change, to its status, to its shape and size, to its capacity, to outside influences. The School passed through all these 'tests' with honour, closure had never loomed, and why – because of the strong and effective leadership that has always prevailed. I quote leadership rather than management – you can 'manage' your car, you can 'manage' your diary, you can 'manage' your house, they never answer back. Managing people is different – they invariably do answer back – people need 'leading', and at Rickmansworth School, a people orientated institution, there has always been effective management, and strong leadership. That is why the school is where it is today – effective, respected and long-lasting; it has survived the Fifty Golden Years with great credit.

A roll call of both the chairmen of the governors, headmasters and headmistresses, serves as a reminder of why the school has been so effective and stable since it was founded in 1953.

The first three chairmen of the governors, from Colonel C.E. Goad MC in 1954, to County Councillors A. Peebles and Mrs. V.M. Dulonty BA, steered the school through its first 30 years. They were followed by Mrs. K. Mendelsson MBE, who guided the school through the following two decades and two changes in status before handing over the reins in 1998 to the current chairman, Dr. J.E. Anderson.

Both the late Peter Morrill and the late Miss Mildred Collings lead the school through its first twenty years until 1974, as both the first headmaster and headmistress respectively. Hugh Forsyth followed on for an unprecedented 26 years at the top until his retirement in 2000 when the current headmaster, Dr. Stephen Burton took up the role. Mrs. Marit Sargint (nee Edwards) became headmistress after 'Millie' until 1988 before handing on to Mrs. Christine Titus, who in turn in 2000 passed the reins to the present incumbent, Mrs. Marija Ullman. The fact that there have in fifty years only been three headmasters and four headmistresses is a reflection of the success of the school. They all stuck to their task amidst tumultuous changes, and lead from the front.

Throughout those years the headmasters and headmistresses were ably supported by a succession of deputy headmasters – Tom Davies, Peter Rowland, Graham Heddle, Peter Stowe, Hugh Forsyth, Stan Goodman and currently Tim Griffiths.

Millie Collings

By the late fifties Countess Mountbatten had accepted the honour of becoming the first Patron of the school, being succeeded by Lady Bowes-Lyon after her death some years later.

A reflection on both Millie Collings and Peter Morrill will show just how they exerted their own influence and set their standards on the school during those first twenty years. Millie's tribute that follows was written by her nephew Richard Gallimore and shows how she, as a great lady, commanded respect second to none. Peter Morrill was ——well—— Peter Morrill, an enigma, a man remembered by all, in many various ways, well summed up in the anecdotes of former teachers and pupils later in this book, and the short tribute that follows.

Presentation plate to Mille

Mildred Lucy Collings – Headmistress 1954 to 1974

A keen musician, and a gifted pianist and violinist, who could have made a career for herself on the concert platform, instead she devoted herself to teaching.

Among her many attributes were a high intellectual ability, firmness, organising power and tactful understanding of others' weaknesses. She became the first Headmistress of Rickmansworth Grammar School after already having led an eventful life.

From 1919 to 1926 she attended the County Secondary School, Streatham, gaining a Draper's Company Scholarship and passing the higher school examination in Latin, English, French and Modern History, with distinctions in Latin and English. In 1926 she entered the Royal Holloway College where she received an honours in Latin and a first in Greek. She also made a great study in Greek, which was to prove so useful in her love of the classics and the classical age.

She began her teaching career in 1930 at Farnborough Grammar School, and then in 1936 she spent a year at the Portsmouth Northern Grammar School for girls in order to gain wider experience. In 1937 she became Senior Mistress at the County High School, Brockenhurst, Hampshire, busying herself even more during the war when she spent frequent nights on watch duties.

In 1951 she became Senior Mistress at Rye Grammar School in East Sussex and Senior House Mistress, Saltcote Place, a boarding school house for forty girls. She was appointed Headmistress of Rickmansworth Grammar School when the new premises were opened in 1954. This was the start of a very long and successful professional association with the late Peter Morrill, and with South West Hertfordshire Education Authority.

Everyone has their own personal recollection of Miss Collings in and out of school. She proved to be a tireless figure, constantly urging and encouraging pupils and colleagues to even greater efforts for the benefit of themselves and the school. To encourage pupils and staff she opened her nearby home at a very early stage for extra curricula music lessons, given by herself and Mr Arch. From the first contact, she came across just as she was, a dedicated supremely competent teacher. One was always suddenly aware of one's speech and grammar, and whether one's shoes were polished and one's hair combed. She was someone who demanded high standards of herself and others, a teacher who insisted on her pupils developing their talents to the full, a person who never ceased to learn from life, in all a woman of integrity and courage, a very independent minded person.

She retired in 1975 but continued teaching in a voluntary capacity, especially at St. Joan of Arc, where, she would lead a variety of classes and help run the library.

Apart from teaching she was also closely involved with St. John's Primary School as well as St. Joan's Convent in the capacity as Clerk to the Governors. Among her many voluntary activities was collecting for good causes, including the Lifeboat Fund, Save the Children, the Blind and especially for Michael Sobell House at Mount Vernon. When she was in her eighties she and Peter Morrill made an epic travel holiday by train through Europe down to Sicily and back. Even after being 'mugged' whereby she lost her handbag, passport and currency it did not deter her enthusiasm for travel. On many occasions she and Peter would take advantage of British Rail offers of day trips. On more than one occasion they did a day trip from London to Edinburgh, complete with thermos flasks and sandwiches. Two or three times a year the two of them would travel down to Gloucestershire by train to see Isabell Parfett, who was the school's first bursar. Until 1993 she was still taking pupils up to A-level for Latin, English and French.

Her energy seemed inexhaustible, her enthusiasm tireless and keenness to help others unquenchable. She will be long remembered.

Peter Morrill – Headmaster 1953-1974

Peter Morrill, the school's first headmaster, as mentioned more than many times, developed a reputation that to this day has never been forgotten. Tall, austere, dominant, he was a man who drove by example, though many of his ways may have been construed more than mildly eccentric, to say the least.

After the war he had gained a headship in 1947 at the British Military School, Wilhelmshaven, and a post war military garrison town on the north coast of West Germany. British forces were still in occupation as a result of the surrender terms at the end of the war, and would remain so for many more decades as a result of NATO's commitment to the "cold war" that then hung over Europe.

Peter Morrill

Schooling for the children of servicemen's families living in Germany was a necessity and Peter Morrill played his part in it, gaining the very vision of proper schooling that he was to adopt in his later years.

In 1953 Peter Morrill had accepted the post of Headmaster of the new Rickmansworth Grammar School, but his dream of starting in the new premises in September was thwarted – the construction work at Scots Hill was not finished. He therefore accepted the dual role of Headmaster of 'two' schools – Rickmansworth – and the newly built secondary modern school in Oxhey – Clarendon. It was a unique start to twenty one years of a never to be forgotten Headship.

From the outset he adopted principles that nothing but the best was required for the name of Rickmansworth Grammar School, he intended the school to equal that of his long established rivals – Merchant Taylor's, the Royal Masonic and Watford Boys and Girls Grammar School.

Though teachers and pupils were all individuals, Peter Morrill derived a real family feeling amongst everyone. He came from Germany, where his brief had been to 'eliminate the D-stream mentality'. He brought that aim to Ricky, and tried to make it difficult for children to compare their attainment with others. All indicators of streaming and setting were hidden, after the first year at Clarendon School form orders, ranking in exams, streaming, 'moving up' or 'moving down' were eliminated, though even to this day it is difficult to avoid as such, we all have a competitive streak in us, and though it was contained in the classrooms at Ricky, it was fully encouraged on the sports field – as it still is – despite all the varied attempts to stop it there over the last fifty years.

Peter Morrill believed in the importance of morning assembly, much is said elsewhere about the sanctity of the school hall floor and footwear thereof, but it was in his eyes in those days an important part of school life to attend morning worship before going about the day's business. Though this philosophy may have changed many years later where the act of worship should be voluntary, compelling pupils was considered demeaning, then there was only one practised religion in the school – Christianity, with the preponderance being Church of England. Nowadays modern thinking sees morning religious assembly as inappropriate within the multi-cultural society that we now live in. Assembly at Ricky ensured at one point in the day the whole school was together in one place.

Peter Morrill, despite his fierce appearance around the school, was a kind and caring man. He firmly believed in the values of discipline, honesty and courtesy, woe betide any pupil who did not meet with his expectations. He always maintained an innermost concern for the welfare of all those at the school, be they members of staff, or pupils. If someone had a problem – then this took precedence over all else. Pupils quickly learned this, when he could not be found after school to take an important telephone call from 'above', it was safe to assume he was helping a pupil hunt for a lost book, or gym shoe. Those words of his successor, Hugh Forsyth, sum up the man that Peter Morrill was, strict, pupil orientated, kind, understanding, a good judge of character, trusting of his staff and eccentric with it all too! He was firm but fair – good manners were important, many a potential new teacher would be judged at interview when Millie Collings entered the room – if they stood up, they were 'in', if they remained seated, that was 'curtains'!

7 – The 'Management'

Maybe he will be most remembered for two things, his obsession with litter and an often used morning assembly phrase – "he has been caned". As described in some later anecdotes, the dropping of litter was 'verboten'. Such an act of disgraceful behaviour would be severely dealt with, but if the culprit was not caught, Peter Morrill would be there to clear it up; this is probably summed up best in the adopted school prayer – "help with joy to any task for others"!

The Peter Morrill Centre Block

To sum up, Peter Morrill's legacy lived on well after he left, and nothing more fitting can be said than to see the words 'THE PETER MORRILL CENTRE' greet everyone as they enter the school gates. He was an enigma, and in his own immortal words "I want to make it crystal clear" – and crystal clear he was, we all knew where we stood with him, I guess he will never be forgotten.

NISI COLLAPSUM ERIT

8

A HEADMASTER'S OVERVIEW

Hugh Forsyth

Hugh Forsyth, who led the school through two of its three status changes in 1990 and 1999 and was deputy headmaster from 1969 before becoming headmaster in 1974 during the transition to comprehensive status, has 'falteringly' produced his personal overview that follows of those 26 years he served the school as headmaster.

> *Former pupils and staff returning to the school after a gap of many years frequently remark on how familiar it is, and how little change seems to have occurred. The buildings they knew so well are still there and largely unchanged. There have been significant additions since the early days, and some modifications to use, by and large things seem much the same. They see only the surface of course, or do they sense something else?*
>
> *I was fortunate to serve under Peter Morrill as deputy headmaster for four years before being appointed his successor when he and Miss Collings retired in 1974. Despite his fierce appearance around the school he was a kind and caring man. His concern for the individual has remained at the centre of the school's values over the past 30 year and is one of the core elements that drove it during my time.*
>
> *There have however been big changes during that time. The change from a small grammar school of 600 pupils to an all-ability school of 1200 was the most significant. The increase in the number of pupils began shortly after the school opened, reflected in the science/dining wing extension built as early as 1961, and followed during the sixties by the sixth form block and CDT block (those horrid grey asbestos panels), and the acquisition of Scots Hill Court, that delightful old Victorian mansion at the top of Scots Hill, which became the home of the art and music departments until its loss in a fire during the early seventies. As the numbers*

of pupils and staff continued to grow the 'new science' block was added, connected by an unusual bridge structure to the main building, and the music block to replace the loss of Scots Hill Court, both in 1974. The art department had to remain behind in old mobile classrooms in the garden of Scots Hill Court for twenty years because Hertfordshire had under-insured Scots Hill Court.

The development from a selective grammar school to an all-ability school (I find 'comprehensive' an ugly term with bad connotations) was a challenge for us in the 1970s, and although there were some staff with misgivings there was a strong will overall to make it succeed. Our plan was to retain the academic standard and ethos whilst extending the curricular provision for the wider ability range. We were determined, in the first place, that the most able would not be disadvantaged in any way. Looking back, I believe that group also benefited from the new opportunities available to them. Secondly, the high standards of personal conduct and our School values would support the integration of the 'new' intake of boys and girls.

There were some difficult times at first, caused largely by the rapid increase in size of the School. The form unit and our practice of each pupil remaining in the same form throughout their school life needed a structure to support and co-ordinate the larger numbers, and so the Year groups were introduced. The school was divided into four groups by age: first and second forms (lower school), third and fourth forms (middle school), fifth form and sixth form. Senior staff were chosen to lead them, and the stage was set to develop the pastoral system based on the form unit that was the key ingredient in the school's pupil progress and welfare arrangements.

For the next fifteen years there were no new buildings or significant investment in the School by Hertfordshire. There was need, but our requests, pleas and demands all fell on deaf ears. Meanwhile, the accommodation deteriorated, the temporary classrooms wheeled in as emergency measures became permanent, and we struggled to provide our pupils with the resources they deserved. Hertfordshire became preoccupied with managing the national decline in the school populations and propping up struggling schools. Schools such as Rickmansworth that were popular with parents were starved of funds to keep open schools that should have been closed. The lifeline during those years was the Parents Guild.

The Parents Guild was set up during Peter Morrill's time, and their first major project was the swimming pool. During the eighties in particular, when the school could no longer look to Hertfordshire for investment, the guild laboured away raising funds through the covenant scheme, the uniform shop, fetes, fairs, jumble sales, social events and so on, to provide us with many important resources. Apart from the first computer suite and the careers suite, during that time they funded many 'essentials' such as Hall chairs, stage curtains, computers and musical instruments. The 'guild' has been a huge source of support for the school during the past 30 years, and I made good friends amongst the parents through the guild. Many parents continued their support long after their children left the school, and some became the governors I came to depend on in the later years.

The nineties were the most significant years for the school during my time. Having neglected the school since the early seventies, in 1988 Hertfordshire came to ask for our cooperation in return for which they offered a new art building – nearly twenty years late. They had closed William Penn School in Rickmansworth and now were at last taking on the closure of Durrants in Croxley Green. Their plan was to merge us with Durrants, running a split site school until the number of pupils declined to the point when they would all fit onto the Rickmansworth site. Despite the desperate need for new buildings we turned down the proposal because we believed it would not benefit the existing pupils and their successors. Hertfordshire attempted to impose their will regardless of our view we took an option that the Conservative Government had recently introduced: we applied for grant-maintained status, or as the step was called at the time we 'opted out'. In 1990 Rickmansworth School became the 29th grant-maintained school in the country, the first in Hertfordshire.

It was a democratic decision, reached via a ballot of parents. Hertfordshire opposed the application, but there was a clear majority of parents in favour, despite the fears Hertfordshire attempted to create. It was certainly a step into the unknown, but as with most pilot schemes it was well supported by the government of the day. For us it was an exciting and rewarding period. We had moved overnight from a school 100% maintained and controlled by Hertfordshire County Council to an independent school within the maintained sector. There were two big benefits; new funds for running the school and the freedom to decide our own future. The 'extra' funds were what Hertfordshire had 'top-sliced' for its administration and supply of central services to the school – most of which we didn't want. Most of these funds were immediately deployed straight into the classroom in the form of teachers and teaching materials.

Thanks to grant-maintained status the school enjoyed a period of dramatic improvement and development during the nineties. Capital grant was obtained for a new art building and for rebuilding the old CDT block, transforming it into a modern technology centre, and the new buildings were opened by Lady Mountbatten, whose mother had opened the school in 1956. Many other improvements were made to the building, but more significantly there was a new optimism and a new sense of pride and achievement in the school, which was shared by pupils, staff, parents and governors. It came from a feeling of ownership and the consequent ability to make things happen.

This is a very personal 'over-view' of the school during my time, and I am conscious that I have not made reference to any of the many people – pupils, staff, parents and governors – who made it what it was. The school of course is them, but that is beyond the scope of this short piece. Perhaps, another time. . . .?

9

THE HOUSE SYSTEM

It has been tradition since time immemorial to subdivide a school into separate 'houses'. It gives pupils something to identify themselves with, together with providing a team basis for competitiveness, particularly in internal school work, sports, competitions, quizzes etc. As soon as pupils arrived on their very first day as fresh faced eleven year olds they were allocated to their house. The sense of rivalry was instilled from day one.

Rickmansworth Grammar School followed the tradition in true spirit, not just calling the houses Red, Blue, Green, Yellow, which is not uncommon, but honouring local distinguished dignitaries of years past gone. The area was flush with connections to such famous personages that the school was spoilt for choice.

There may not have been any pecking order in the choice of names, but an underlying rivalry soon built up as to which was the senior house! There never was one, but they were normally named in the order Caius, Carey, Penn and Anson and the pecking order, whilst instilling 'friendly rivalry' was actually based on the dates of birth of each of the four persons after whom they were named, the oldest first!

With the school originally planned as four separate blocks, it did not take the mathematicians long to put two and two together, come up with four, and do the obvious thing – name each of the four blocks after one of the four house names. It was not to be a test of pupil domesticity to see who could keep their 'block' the tidiest, on many occasions the headmaster himself undertook this, but it did give pupils an identity to a part of the building, and not just a name. Those four houses and their respective block are as follows:-

Caius House, named after Dr. John Keys, 1510-1573. His name is pronounced in the English way but usually written in the Latin form. He studied medicine at Cambridge, and was physician to King Edward VI (the boy king), Queen Mary Tudor, and to Queen Elizabeth the First, who rewarded him in 1557 with the Manor of Croxley Hall and Parrott's Farm on Croxley Green. He rebuilt his old college (Gonville) and endowed the college with the two arms which still today belong to Gonville and Caius College. Caius House colour was green, and adopted school area was the science block.

Carey House, named after Sir Robert Carey, 1570 – 1639, who served as a volunteer against the Spanish Armada. When Queen Elizabeth the First died at Richmond on Thames, his sister, who was a lady-in-waiting to the Queen, dropped her ring out of the window as a signal that the Queen was dead. Sir Robert rode with it to Edinburgh in two and a half days and gave it to King James the Sixth of Scotland, who a few days later was proclaimed James the First of England. Sir Robert was made Earl of Monmouth and built Monmouth House, which still stands in Watford High Street. Carey House colour was blue, and adopted school area was the gymnasium and dining room block – now the Peter Morrill Centre.

Penn House, *named after William Penn, 1644-1718, a Quaker who lived in Basing House in Rickmansworth. He was given a grant of land in 1681 in North America by King Charles the First in payment for money that the King had borrowed from Penn's father. The land was called Pennsylvania and many Quakers emigrated there from this country. William Pem later returned to England, dying 1718 and is buried at Jordans near Rickmansworth. Penn House colour was yellow and adopted school area was the assembly hall and administration block.*

Anson House, *named after Admiral Sir George Anson, 1697-1762, who sailed round the world in pursuit of the Spanish navy, captured half a million pounds' worth of treasure and bought the big house at Moor Park with the proceeds. After defeating the French Navy off Cape Finisterre he was made First Lord of the Admiralty and reconstituted the Royal Marines. Anson House colour was red and adopted school area the main classroom block.*

A room in each of the four 'house blocks' was designated for pupils to hold house meetings in; however even from the early days the frequency of such occasions was rare! – if not unheard of! In comparison sporting rivalry was unquestionable, be it on the rugby, hockey, netball or rounders fields, or more particularly at the annual school sports day. Old traditions did not 'die hard', whatever competition it was, pupils proudly identified themselves to their house.

10

THE SCHOOL'S STATUS – FOUR CHANGES IN FIFTY YEARS

From its founding in 1953 Rickmansworth School maintained its grammar school status for the next sixteen years, until 1969 when the government decreed it was to become a comprehensive school; however the transition to this new status was phased to take place over the succeeding five years.

Comprehensive schooling ordained that selective education would be replaced by a non-selective all ability system. The first such intake started in 1969 and as 'selected' intakes from the old grammar system left, they were replaced by the new 'all ability' ones. By 1974 the main school was fully comprehensive with the first five years based on all ability intakes but with the sixth form still retaining a selected intake status.

Over the years this status has been confused, sometimes referred to as comprehensive, sometimes as maintained. A comprehensive school is normally understood to mean a school with pupils not selected by academic ability, whilst a maintained school is a state school, or a school maintained by the state, regardless of whether it is selective or not. In effect all schools maintained from public funds are (state) maintained. Rickmansworth School remained officially in the category of 'county maintained' by Hertfordshire Local Education Authority (LEA) until the late eighties. Throughout this time the Governors of the school were responsible to the Secretary of State for Education for all aspects of the school's activities. Confused – yes!

By 1989, with William Penn School in Mill End closed and Durrants School in Croxley likely to follow the same fate, the County Council suggested that Rickmansworth School should merge with Durrants instead. Their bargaining chip was the offer to fund the building of a new arts block, on the condition that the merger took place.

The merger was rejected by Rickmansworth School – mainly over two problems; one, of it becoming a 'split site', which it was felt would cause damage to the education at both schools; and two, the fact that the county council had failed to address problems foreseen over staffing of the schools. On 20th March 1989 the school governors formally rejected the 'offer'.

In July 1989, a ballot was taken with the 1,023 parents of all the pupils to determine whether or not an application should be made to the Secretary of State for Education to change status again and become a Grant-Maintained School instead. A favourable majority agreed that the application should be made.

In July 1990 the Secretary of State notified his intention to approve the change to Grant-Maintained status, effective from 1st September that year. Durrants School was not therefore merged and finally closed.

As a Grant-Maintained School, Rickmansworth was immediately able to obtain those much needed funds to run the school, with money coming direct from the Department of Education and Science by way of an Annual Maintenance Grant (AMG). The responsibility for control and expenditure for such schools was invested in the Board of Governors, and not Hertfordshire County Council. It was felt that such status would prove more beneficial to Rickmansworth School. Most ties with the county council were severed as a result. Major new building projects were funded and completed in the nineties under the system, all being crucial to the future of the school.

However, new government legislation in 1999 decreed that Rickmansworth School would change its status yet again and for the fourth time in 46 years. It would cease to be a Grant-Maintained School, and in September that year would become a Foundation School. Funding would be allocated by the Department of Education via the Local Education Authority (LEA), in this case Herts County Council (again!).

It is pertinent to copy an extract from the Governors' Annual Report to parents in July 1999, which highlights the anticipated effects of the change of status to Foundation School.

> *The new government's legislation on schools is now having its effects. The school will cease to be Grant Maintained on August 31st and will become a Foundation School. The school's nine years as Grant Maintained have seen considerable changes that governors are sure are for the better. Now, the Local Education Authority will play a somewhat greater role in the future of the school, but by no means as large as ten years ago. We will seek to benefit from what the L.E.A. has to offer. One particularly striking point is that in spite of the Education Secretary having convinced most people that there is real extra money – beyond inflation – for schools in the coming year; most schools' budgets are down in real terms. The money is not getting past the L.E.A. to the schools, certainly not to Rickmansworth School, where next year, the pupil/teacher ratio will be the highest for many years.*
>
> *The sums the governors can budget for items further from the core of the school's activities, for property maintenance, or for future development, have been cut much more drastically, and this is a major reason why we have decided to set up a School Foundation as a focus for a new sort of fund-raising. The Parents Guild has most successfully combined money-raising and social activities over many years, and will continue to do so. The government will henceforth run the parents' covenant scheme, intending to raise its profile so we can credibly ask outsiders to do their share of funding future projects. The Foundation will be the initial destination for such monies, and you will all inevitably hear more about this soon.*
>
> *One consequence of the new act for the governing body is that there will be more of us. There are two further parent governors who have just been elected, two governors to be nominated by the L.E.A., and a governor elected by the non-teaching staff of the school.*
>
> *The other area where changes may emerge is in our admissions criteria for selecting pupils for transfer from primary school. Rickmansworth School is a very popular choice among parents facing this transfer for their children, so we cannot admit all those who want to come. Invidious though the process is, we have to select. Successive governments have obliged governing bodies to change their criteria for the process – we have never sought to change criteria ourselves.*
>
> *When a school is oversubscribed, all admissions criteria have disadvantages, and different criteria lead to a different set of disappointed parents. It may suit politicians to argue over which group of parents shall be disappointed and devise criteria accordingly, but your governors are not inclined to social experiments. We are certainly uncomfortable about public discussion of the matter with those who have an explicitly political agendum. We therefore prefer criteria which aim to maintain the present character of the school, and hope that they will be accepted and we will be judged on that basis. We are, I believe realistic about 'the present character' rather than smug.*

10 – The School'S Status – Four Changes in Fifty Years

> *Finally, the governors recognise that their particular contribution to the school can look good only in the reflected light of the great efforts of the teaching and other staff and the head teacher and his deputies. The strength of support of parents is also of great importance to the overall outcome so we thank you and all these for contributing.*

In a century where education was finally taken by the 'scruff of the neck' by successive governments, knocked somewhat into shape, then altered for the bad, and altered for the good, and back again, Rickmansworth School survived.

As a Foundation School, Rickmansworth is self-governing, with the governing body responsible for the employment of staff, admission of pupils together with all aspects of the organisation and running of the school.

Originally only built to last for sixty years, it is on course to continue for at least another fifty years – and probably many more, though no doubt there will be another one, or more, status changes along that route.

Near the end of the fifty golden years in 2002, Rickmansworth was designated as DfES Specialist Arts College, focusing on the Performing Arts, thus allowing the school to build on its academic, extra curricular and traditional strengths, broadening pupils' experience and opportunities. Official recognition of this status was conferred in September 2003. Today the school is also leading a DfES Schools Sports Partnership with links to national sports governing bodies and 45 local schools.

11

SIX DECADES OF NATIONAL HISTORY

As the country slowly recovered from the ravages of the World War, each of the succeeding decades could be identified in their own significant and separate ways. The fifties were a frugal era, money was sparse, food was in short supply, one made do with what one had. You made your own fun – there was little by way of help to assist. In the sixties life began to swing, recovery was a thing of the past and by the seventies the platform for the boom years of the eighties and nineties was laid.

No history, not even that of Rickmansworth School would be complete without recording the milestones of those decades. A mere pause for reflection over some of the occurrences will highlight the way our lives have been influenced by them during the last fifty years, how school life was duly guided decade by decade and how the development of humanity – us – has been affected forever.

The Frugal Fifties

Whilst the Korean War, the Mau Mau Emergency, Suez, Hungary, Cyprus, the Cold War all played havoc with family life, fathers being away on duty, many as National Servicemen, children were brought up almost as one parent families. A number of major events made an enormous impact on life during this time. The accession of Queen Elizabeth to the throne, the launching of the first spacecraft, 'sputnik', in 1957, the Conquest of Everest, the H-Bomb, the dawning of the Rock 'n Roll Era, and Britain's joining of EFTA (European Free Trade Association) were amongst them.

But whilst there were National or even international events of significance, domestic

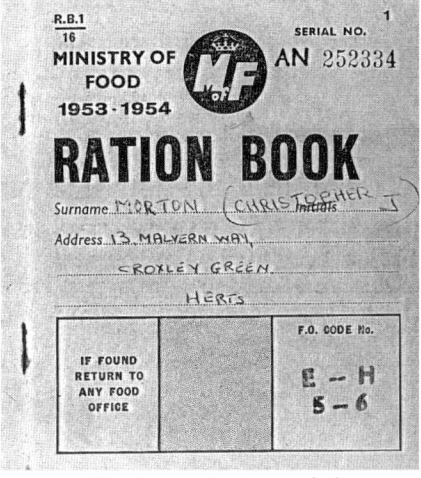

Wartime rationing ended

changes were abound – Zebra Crossings, Yellow Lines, Parking Meters, Motorways, Hovercraft – all came about and were destined to affect our lives 'on the move' forever! On the radio the first and longest running 'soap' started – the Archers – replacing Dick Barton Special Agent – and BBC TV found itself a direct rival with Commercial Television in the form of ITV, with the very first advert – for Gibbs SR toothpaste – appearing.

The music industry was in swing and by 1952 the very first 'Popular Singles Charts' were produced, with American singer Al Martino recording the first ever "Number One". Once unheard of, Hippy, psychedelic and non-U became common language.

Even as far back as the fifties, Postal Codes were introduced – mainly experimental – but a forerunner to us being found nowadays not so much by an address – but by yet another identifying number! Most people can nowadays be identified by up to twenty different numbers!

Premium Bonds were introduced; the Miss World Contest had its first outing, Teddy Boys made their appearance and impact on Society, and Wartime Rationing finally ended. It was the decade in which DNA was first discovered – the building blocks of life – but not realised at the time how significant a discovery it would be.

In 1954 the Four Minute Mile was finally broken – by a Briton no less – Roger Bannister, as another Briton, Diane Leather became the first woman to break five minutes over the same distance and the victorious Manchester United Football team suffered severe losses at the Munich Air Crash in 1958.

The Burgess, Maclean and Philby defections rocked the British Establishment as much as the Piltdown Man did when his remains were found to be a hoax – his teeth gave him away!

On a sad front Britain suffered nearly 5,000 deaths through unforeseen tragedies – the London smog, the East coast storms, Lynton / Lynmouth flash flood, the sinking of Stranraer Car Ferry and tragic rail crashes at Harrow and Lewisham.

And so the era ended with those old favourites 'fish and chips' now costing 1/- (5p) and a 'pint', for those qualified of course, a staggering 10d (4p).

The Swinging Sixties

As we rolled into a new decade, deemed nationally as the best decade for music and fashion, the world was changing, some international events were to have a profound and instant effect on the development of the decade, others were to roll on over a number of years, often with devastating effects.

The Cuban Missile Crisis, Russia's first cosmonaut – Yuri Gagarin, the assassinations of John F. Kennedy, Dr. Heindrich Verwoed and Martin Luther King and the first man to land on the moon had a near instant effect on world life.

The Berlin Wall, South Africa's withdrawal from the British Empire & Commonwealth because of its Apartheid policies, UDI in Rhodesia in 1965, the Vietnam War and the Czechoslovak uprising in 1968 all brought long term strife and endless repercussions.

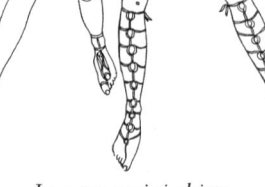

In came mini skirts

At home in 1963 the country was hit by a triple blow with the Profumo Affair, the Great Train Robbery, and phasing out of steam traction from the railways, with the closure of nearly 50% of the rail network.

Britain's attempt to expand their EFTA membership to full membership of the EEC was twice blocked by the infamous "Nons" from France.

The first TV Soap appeared in 1961 via Manchester's Coronation Street and the most famous names of the era, the Beatles, from neighbouring Liverpool, were to hit the national and world scene with a razzmatazz never seen before, their influence in popular music remains number one even today.

The simmering "Irish problem", first at a head in 1916, exploded in 1968, and continues today.

On the roads, cars were becoming more plentiful as affluence made its mark in society "you

11 – Six Decades of National History

have never had it so good" came the PM's infamous statement, and coupled with this came the first MOT tests, the first breathalyser, 70 mile per hour speed limits, topped off by huge rises in fuel prices.

The mini skirt, courtesy of Mary Quant, became "the fashion", youngsters revelling in the break from Victorian stodginess – now with their ability to say "their piece" as the voting age was reduced from twenty-one to eighteen. Betting shops were legalised, off shore Commercial Radio appeared, but was not legalised.

Frances Chichester completed the first single-handed round the world yacht trip in 1967, North Sea oil was discovered, the two tier mail system (first/second mail class) was introduced and Britain's first satellite was launched. As another new era dawned with the successful maiden flight of Concorde, old eras disappeared – national service ended and the death penalty was abolished.

On a low, the tragedy at Aberfan will never be forgotten any more than the devastation to the Cornish coastline and wildlife with the Torrey-Canyon Disaster.

On a high, England beat their old foes West Germany in the final of soccer's World Cup at Wembley. The wait however for a similar triumph was to go on for another 37 years!

The Stormy Seventies

Stormy – because they were the era of the hippies, drop outs, radicals, demonstrators, activists, and free speaking, an accumulation of extremes of freedom now enjoyed by the human race.

It was a decade of turmoil; Britain struggled heavily under both the Irish problem and the "Cold" War, America more so under Vietnam. It was a time of people unrest – the postal strike, the miners' strike, the refuse collection strike, the firemen's strike, the year-long Times Newspaper strike. They took their toll, none less than a toppled government. In America Watergate beat a President.

A thousand years of heritage goes overnight – decimal coins replace £sd – this £1.18.6¼, ten separate denominations made up of 32 coins and 1 note becomes £1.94 in today's money!

Disasters abound included the Dutch Elm Disease – sixteen million trees destroyed, thalidomide, the Ibrox Football Stadium and Moorgate Underground tragedies, the Munich Olympics Massacre, the Soweto Riots – beamed by television worldwide – and Lord Mountbatten's murder.

Decimalised currency was finally introduced – replacing the old Pounds, Shillings and Pence, our system for a thousand years – reluctantly accepted, now normal. How did we cope with a currency baseline of "twelve", and not "ten"? Only "us" oldies will remember!

Uganda, under Idi Amin, expelled 40,000 Asians; with nowhere to go they brought their culture to Britain. North Sea Oil came ashore for the first time; the dreaded VAT appeared, as did the first "MacDonald's". The fast food era had begun.

In contrast we shivered as snow fell during the first week of June 1975, only to find us basking in the heat wave of the century exactly a year later in 1976, and with no rainfall in two and a half months this led to the worst drought for five hundred years as reservoirs dried up and water was severely rationed – "bath with a friend" was the call of the day. Britain was not prepared!

The country basked in the glory of the Queen's Silver Jubilee in 1977 and a rare win through Virginia Wade to coincide at the Women's Final at Wimbledon.

The "Nons" were over as Britain, accompanied by Ireland, were finally accepted as members of the EEC. After the Wimbledon triumph, ladies remained to the fore – Margaret Thatcher, already dubbed "The Iron Lady" by Moscow – became Britain's first woman Prime Minister and Louise Brown became the world's first test tube baby.

Vietnam ended, the pundits wondering what it ever achieved, discussions around a table ten years earlier would have achieved the same result without the catastrophic loss of life, and Britain's colonial thorn, UDI, ended in Rhodesia – as it became the new independent state of Zimbabwe.

The Pop Group Abba became Sweden's biggest foreign exchange earner; and the new era of everlasting (to this day) Christmas hit records was ushered in by the decade's top British group – Slade.

The Affluent Eighties

If Britain swung in the sixties, and endured tempestuous times in the seventies, the eighties, the coolest decade ever – weather wise that is – was an era of boom, in two senses; firstly, through stability and prosperity amongst the population who were enjoying an upsurge, and secondly, in contrast with conflict and disaster hitting an unprecedented high.

1982 was dominated by the Falkland's Conflict – Britain showed the world that the impossible, could be overcome – don't mess with us we said! It followed hard on the heels of the Iran Embassy hostage crisis, only to be followed closely a couple of years later by the Grand Hotel bombing in Brighton and the Libyan Air Raids.

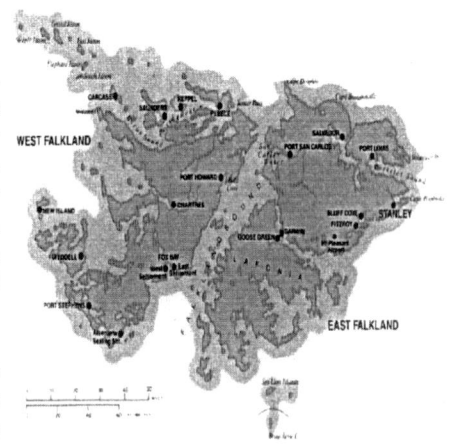

The Falklands Crisis

The decade of disasters can only be described through the loss of one thousand two hundred people as a result of two North Sea Oil Rig fires, serious football stadium tragedies (Bradford, Hillsborough and Heysel), three rail disasters (Purley, Kings Cross and Clapham), a multiple crash on the newly opened M25 motorway, the Hungerford shootings, a serious outbreak of Legionnaires Disease, the toppling of the Herald of Free Enterprise Ferry off Zeebrugge and two air crashes – Kegworth near the M1, and lastly – Lockerbie – enough said.

If we add the environmental havoc caused by the sudden (almost) unexpected Hurricane in October 1987 in south-east England, when fifteen million trees were brought down, it was a wretched decade in terms of loss.

11 – Six Decades of National History

Not all was gloom in the eighties, the 'Coe/Ovett/Cram' era of athletics brought the crowds back to the sport – and very often to their feet as they watched our Olympic heroes reel off victories at Commonwealth, European, World and Olympic Championships – and between all three of them breaking the World Mile Record on six successive occasions, three of them within a span of only nine days.

The Chernobyl Nuclear Reactor, deep inside the USSR, exploded in 1986, Mikhail Gorbachev exploded the Soviet Communist theory that ended with the dissolution of the USSR, the collapse of Communism and the fall of the Berlin Wall, the latter paradoxically after Rudolph Hess's death in jail in Berlin and with the seemingly impregnable hundred and ten miles of concrete being demolished almost overnight – a thought unheard of since it was built in 1961!

On Britain's roads, wearing of seat belts became compulsory in the front of cars, wheel clamps came out in force, and the (then) world's longest suspension bridge – The Humber Bridge – opened, its great supporting towers further apart at the top than the bottom due to the curvature of the earth!

Urban violence increased with the IRA bombing in London, there were race riots in London, Bristol and Liverpool, the year long Miners' Strike, the Greenham Common Cruise Missile Protests and the Libyan Embassy shooting. The Great Train Robbery was upstaged by the Brinksmat Gold Bullion Robbery, a mere £26 million of gold being snatched.

Whilst Britain recorded its coldest ever day in December 1981, -29.6°C in Shropshire, warnings of Global warming and the Greenhouse effect were being studied more closely.

The City experienced the infamous 'Big Bang' on the Stock Markets, unemployment was rising, council houses were being sold off, the Church of England approved the ordination of women amidst much protest, the Yorkshire Ripper was finally arrested, Tit Bits magazine was issued in 1984, the £1 coin entered circulation and to cap it all, not only were 'Golliwogs' banned, a favourite of children in years gone by, but the very controversial Poll Tax was introduced. This was to see the downfall of a Prime Minister.

The Nervous Nineties

As furious riots over Poll Tax heralded the arrival of the nineties, ironically, voted the worst decade, they also signalled the end in late 1990 of the century's longest serving Prime Minister, Margaret Thatcher, after three terms and eleven years in office.

On the world front, the collapse of Communism had brought about political and social upheaval in a united Germany and right across the former Eastern States to the USSR itself. Some heads 'rolled'. The political map of Europe changed yet once more in this turbulent century, Mikhail Gorbachev went into well-earned retirement.

Africa's thorn, South Africa, finally acceded to the release of former black activist Nelson Mandela, after 27 years in jail. Apartheid was formally abolished in April 1994 and Mr. Mandela became the Republic's first black President. Elsewhere Iraq invaded Kuwait, but the intervention by invitation of the coalition forces reversed the situation in a new form of conflict – missile and electronic warfare. In India President Ranjit Ghandi was assassinated, and in Hong Kong, Britain's ninety-nine year lease finally ended on 30 June, 1997, and the island was handed back to mainland China.

The Poll Tax was replaced by a Community Tax, and accepted, though the yearly rises have been far from enjoyed and the opposite ends of the Channel Tunnel were finally linked up.

An earthquake, epicentre Wrexham, was recorded early in the decade, measuring 5.2 on the Richter scale, the heaviest of the century. Superficial damage was recorded.

The IRA continued their mainland assaults, including one daring attempt on No 10 Downing Street, a glimmer of hope, albeit still a glimmer was reached through the 1998 Good Friday Agreement.

By the end of the decade there were no more than fifty survivors of the Great War (WWI), and the last reunion of the thirty remaining survivors of the Battle of the Somme took place at Thiepual in France.

Britain boasted its first woman Astronaut in 1991 at the same time as the savage imports from the USA – Pit Bull Terriers – were banned.

And the 'Wall' come down as Communism fell

The Cyclones in the Bay of Bengal continued to wreak havoc on the impoverished nation of Bangladesh as 100,000 perished in one violent storm alone.

A rail crash near Paddington Station claimed 31 lives, as storms caused devastation in the South East with forty six perishing in the heavy rains and wind. In Dunblane, Scotland, a lone killer brought savagery of a new kind at a shooting in the local school.

The untimely death of Diana, Princess of Wales, brought shock and horror upon the world, whilst at the same time its back was turned on the genocide in Rwanda-Burundi, brought about by inter tribal hatred of a kind not witnessed in a century. Two million perished.

And now – the Age of Reform

This new era began with the cry from above – reform, reform, reform – what in reality was wrong with the second half of the last century that requires our masters to change it all beggars belief, but here we are, a new century, new ideas, new laws, and a start already beset with turmoil!

Only three years of the first decade of the new millennium passed before Rickmansworth School reached its Golden Jubilee year in 2003.

At the start of those three years, worldwide celebrations saw in the momentous event – not only a departure from the twentieth century, but also from the second millennium. An upsurge in terrorism saw the horrific events in New York in

Mobiles become a way of life

September 2001, the coalition forces hunt for its perpetrators through Afghanistan, the invasion in 2003 of Iraq again led by coalition forces and after a gap of nearly forty years England finally won another World Team Trophy – the William Webb Ellis cup by beating Australia in the World Rugby Championships – in Australia.

Proof of changed times is born out by spiralling inflation hitting our pockets – fish and chips and a pint, still only for those entitled, had each reached a staggering £2.50 – a 5,000% increase in 40 years. *As yer can see i pased me rifmetic an spellin at elefen plus* – by gad sir, have times really changed that much – have I learnt to spell like this from the new 'text message' language that has now invaded our lives?

The Universe, as we know it, distant and not understood, finally came to our TV screens and newspapers, through the sightings from one of man's wonder creations of the last century – the Hubble Telescope. We may after all have alien friends out there, when one day in the future our pocket held mobile phones may even be used to correspond with some distant civilisation. Until then, those two micro spaceship probes – Voyager 1 and Voyager 2 – continue on their space journey, having only in 2003 just left our solar system after nearly twenty years since they left planet earth on their adventure into the big unknown. By the time of Rickmansworth School's Centenary Celebrations in 2053 they may still not have reached our nearest extra terrestrial friend – the star Alpha Centauri. Life has a long way to go!

12

FIFTY YEARS OF ACTION

So much has happened in the first fifty years of Rickmansworth School that to document every minor detail would ensure that you, as the reader, would probably still be reading this by the time of the centenary celebrations in 2053! The major aspects of the development of the school have been covered in other chapters – the concept, the site, the buildings, education, status, sport, drama and music, its management, the school guild to name but a few.

In the following six chapters, each covering one decade in the history of the school, the most significant events are recounted that are not covered in the other chapters. In their own way, each of the six decades has been influenced by the political, social structure and changes that occurred simultaneously during those years. The school in the end is about its staff and pupils, both having been influenced differently as each decade developed and this has been bred into the development of the school. My apologies to pupils for who only an 'initial' instead of a 'full Christian name' appears; in those days documents recorded boys this way whilst girls were afforded their full name.....

TEACHING STAFF

P. J. T. Morrill, B.A.—Headmaster—Modern Languages.
   St. Anselm Hall, Manchester.

Miss M. L. Collings, B.A.—Headmistress—Latin
   Universities of London and Cambridge.

T. C. Davis, B.Sc.—Deputy Headmaster—Biology
   University of Leeds and Carnegie College.

P. G. Rowland, M.A.—Senior English Master
   Wadham College, Oxford.

H. B. Kenyon, Dip. Phys. Ed.—Boys' Physical Education
   Westminster College, and Carnegie College, Leeds

P. W. E. Stowe, B.A.—Geography
   St. Catharine's College, Cambridge.

R. L. Oliver, N.D.D., A.T.D.—Art and Crafts
   University of London.

K. A. Smith, B.Sc., Ph.D., A.R.I.C.—Chemistry
   Imperial College of Science, University of London

Miss T. Y. Troughton, Dip. D.S.—Needlework and Housecraft
   Battersea College of Domestic Science.

Miss S. M. Jeffery, B.A.—French
   Universities of Bristol, Oxford and Paris.

TEACHING STAFF (CONTINUED)

Miss S. F. Thompson, Dip. Phys. Ed.—Girls' Physical Educa
   Dartford College, Kent.

D. J. Drew, B.A.—French
   St. Catherine's College, Oxford, and Un
   Caen, France.

G. Heddle, B.A.—History and Religious Instruction
   St. Edmund Hall, Oxford.

D. J. Owen—Wood and Metal Crafts
   Shoreditch College, London.

E. J. W. Smith, B.Sc.—Mathematics
   University of London.

P. M. Withers, B.Sc.—Mathematics and General Science
   University of London.

G. Arch, B.A.—English and Music
   Selwyn College, Cambridge.

J. C. Spurgeon, B.A.—English and Music
   St. John's College, Cambridge.

A. K. Young, B.Sc.—Mathematics
   University of Wales

Miss Cornell, the Organiser for Light Crafts in the Co
   continue to give help in the teaching of
   Crafts.

Staff roll-call in the early fifties – a motley crew if ever there was!

13

THE FOUNDING FIFTIES – THE DECADE OF 'FIRSTS'

As the school developed from day one in September 1953, it was significant that everything that took place in those early years was a *'first'* at the school. Most of what the pupils of the 1953 and 1954 intakes did and created, as the founding intakes, had not been done before. They, both teachers and pupils, set in place the standards and benchmarks on which the school was based, and latterly evolved.

Many of the Croxley Green domiciled pupils were in themselves unique. From their first day at school in 1946/47 they never went to a school – infants, junior, primary, secondary – with anyone senior to themselves, they were always the founding intake, a phenomenon they carried with them until they left Rickmansworth Grammar School in the late fifties/early sixties. They were indeed a 'rare breed' in education circles.

Those various landmark occasions or achievements – *the firsts* – set by the early intakes at the school are highlighted as and when they occurred in the following paragraphs.

In early 1953 Peter Morrill, PJTM as known to many, was appointed as Headmaster at Clarendon School, whilst also assuming the dual role as the *first* Headmaster of Rickmansworth Grammar School.

At the end of the first term in December 1953, examinations took place and for the *first and only* time marks, grades and class positions were awarded. By the end of the first year the practice ceased, never to be re-instated.

In September 1954 the second intake was enrolled, joining the founding crew on their transfer from Clarendon School to the new Scots Hill site. Though minor construction work was still in progress, these two intakes were not the first to occupy the new premises, since April that year Harvey Road Junior School, itself located only a half a mile away, had taken up usage of four rooms due to their own overcrowding problems. They were to remain at Scots Hill for another couple of years.

The *first* teachers to be appointed joined Peter Morrill at the same time, with Millie Collings assuming the role of headmistress and Tom Davies that of deputy headmaster. The others included Peter Rowland (English), Barry Kenyon (PE), Peter Stowe (Geography), Miss Thelma Troughton (Domestic Science), Miss Stephanie Thompson (PE), David Drew (French), David Owen (Wood and Metal Crafts), Ernie Smith (Maths), Malcolm Withers (Physics), Graham Heddle (History). Many of them had served in the Second World War, often with distinction.

County Alderman Colonel C.E. Goad MC became the *first* Chairman of the School Governors, a post he held until the late fifties and in November 1954 the *first* parents evening was held, with 380 attending and meeting the teachers to discuss the progress of their offspring.

By now the familiar green school uniform was compulsory, worn by both boys and girls with the *first* high street suppliers being Wheatley's in Rickmansworth and Andrew Forbes in Watford. Maroon ties were chosen in memory of the connection with Clarendon School.

The intricacies of 'government' were *first* inflicted on everyone with the end of term enactment of a mock parliament, the founding intake, acting as Cabinet and Opposition and the first year pupils as backbenchers, one wonders how their 'performance' would rate against our 'real life players' of today!

Whilst the bucket and fingernail brigade continued in their quest to de-stone the sports fields (reports elsewhere) so the fledgling sports teams began to take shape in far flung territories such as the Royal Masonic School for Girls, Barton Way Recreation Ground ('rec' as more commonly known), Mill End Playing Fields and the Old Merchants Taylor Rugby Club. By the end of the second year, in the summer of '55, the *first* inter house fixtures were played, but at these faraway venues. The school playing fields were still unfit for use.

Daily Morning Assembly had always been a prominent feature of school activity and it was common for the pupils to 'relax' for a few moments listening to Handel, Bach and Beethoven being played, courtesy of the staff, in the personage of Millie Collings (piano), David Owen (oboe) with songs by Malcolm Withers (baritone) and Stephanie Thompson (soprano).

School lunches, at a princely sum of 1/- per week, were available to all but the Croxley domiciled pupils. On average nearly two hundred pupils ate, joined by their teachers twice a week. Table manners were reported 'to have improved' by the head dinner lady, Mrs. Humphries – were they that bad then? Those Croxley pupils who were deemed to live too close to qualify for the delights of the school's daily cuisine mostly cycled home for a touch of mum's home cooking!

By the end of 1955 the *first* school societies had been formed, including such a diverse range of activities as a Recorder Group, Science Society, Modelling Society (making 'things' that is!), Model Railway Society, a Choir, a Dramatic Society, Christian Union, Geography Club and a Boys Cookery Club.

As many pupils travelled to school by bicycle, a National Police inspired Safe Cycling Test was instigated, and a pass was a prerequisite to being allowed to cycle to school, something necessary even in current times. At the *first* ever tests in 1955, 39 out of 46 pupils passed at the first attempt, two obtaining 98%.

Coincidental with this was the expectation that all school children should be taught to swim, a requirement dating back to civilisations in ancient Grecian and Roman times. The *first* tests were conducted under the scrutiny of National Swimming Coach, Mr. Bill Juba, at Watford Public Baths. Success rate was high and certificates were duly awarded. It is interesting to note that the English were thought to be the first nation in modern society to develop swimming as a sport – probably as early as the turn of the nineteenth century.

In 1956 the *first* 100% attendance record was ever recorded for a school event, the whole school partook in an Ascension Day Church Service at the All Saints Church, opposite the school entrance. This was to become the forerunner of future Annual Founders Day Services.

Following on from this the whole school set foot one morning on another 'collective' trek, this time to Rickmansworth's Picture House Cinema, of frost hollow fame, to watch a special showing of Shakespeare's Henry V. It was much enjoyed by all. This heralded the beginning of drama at the school with the performance of Twelfth Night following soon after – the *first* production ever in the school.

13 – The Founding Fifties – The Decade of 'Firsts'

With the end of term examinations spread over four days, when they were over it was the turn of the Headmaster – no less – to gather the whole school together before the summer break for two days of intensive instruction in a new language on the curriculum – German.

By 1956, excursions of various sorts were becoming a standard feature on the curriculum, starting with the *first* residential adventure away from Scots Hill in the form of a three-day residential Biology Course at the Field Study Centre, Hadham Hall, located eastwards across the wilds of Hertfordshire. Quite how much biology was taught has never been recorded.

Exchange trips with French pupils from Normandy began for the *first* time, a forerunner to future annual excursions; and group trips to seemingly distant beauty spots as the Peak District, set the standard for future, and more adventurous, expeditions to faraway places across the English Channel.

Sport was now making its mark on school affairs, and though rugby and hockey were still played at those more exotic local locations, cricket, tennis and rounders had now found their home on the almost de-stoned school fields. A notable feature of early cricketing days at Barton Way Rec had been the oak tree, situated almost at the start of the bowlers run up – it is still there to this day!

Though not caused by a pupil uprising, the *first* change in school uniform was adopted in 1956 – girls hats were to be made of velour instead of gabardine. Modern fashion was replacing dour Victorian standards.

The main event of the fifties, and one still remembered to this day, was the official opening of the school on 20th June 1956. On a warm clothing, but rain free day, the Rt. Hon Countess Mountbatten of Burma was welcomed by all to Rickmansworth, as she duly declared the 'new' Grammar School 'official'. Extensive outdoor and indoor activities were laid on, all members of staff and pupils being involved. The *first* boat built at the school was christened, quite appropriately, 'Edwina' by the Countess that memorable day and was to feature within days of its launching at the *first* school sponsored sailing competition.

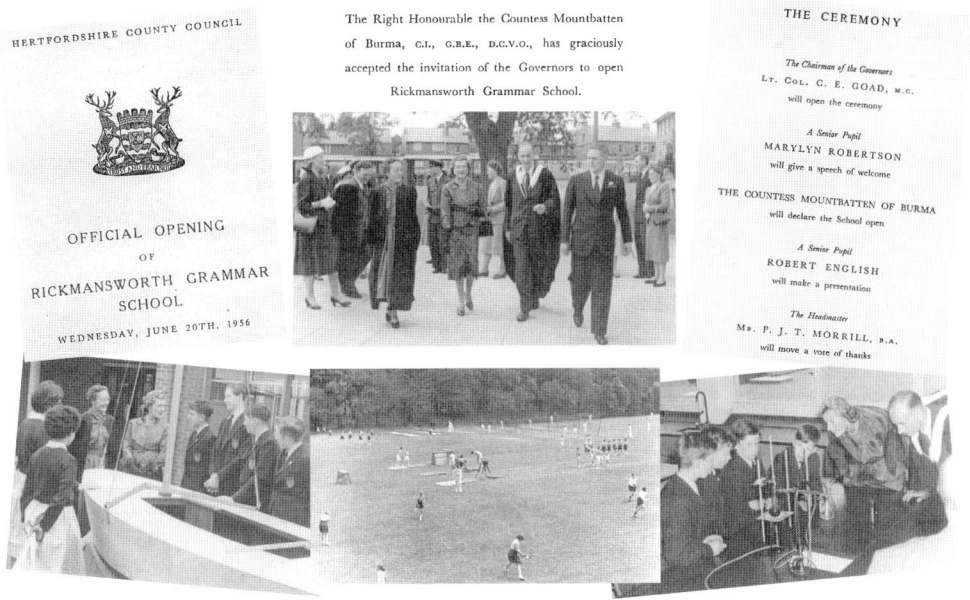

20th June 1956, the school celebrates becoming 'official'

The autumn term that year was greeted by the *first* epidemic to hit the school, 88 pupils were laid low by the national influenza outbreak, and remained off school for a week or more.

By 1957 athletics had made its mark in the school, with several pupils gaining for the *first* time district and county honours on the track and in the field, four of them representing the county at the All England Schools Sports in Durham.

Founders Day, now set firmly in the calendar as the 20th June, was celebrated at All Saints Parish Church for the *first* time, with the whole school, plus the band, sandwiched within its four walls. Later that afternoon what was to be the *first* school sports day, was rained off, the grass track on the sports field resembling a swimming pool. The event took place a week later, when every event winner set a school record – each one in itself being a *first*.

One enjoyable and notorious end of term event was initiated in July 1957 with the *first* practical geography tests taking place. Coach loads of pupils headed off from the school, blindfolded, carrying a map, a sandwich, a drink, a waterproof and one penny in the event of an emergency phone call, being progressively debussed in pairs in the wilds of Hertfordshire and Buckinghamshire, and then told to map read the way back to school. All returned safely, the majority by 6.30 pm, a couple or so a while later, no-one was lost. An event that in today's age may not be so practical – or even allowed!

The school 'coffers' received a small boost as 300 parents from prospective new pupils visited the school, and though their questions were less demanding, their generosity financially exceeded expectations, no record of how much was donated is held.

Service with a smile – the 'Dinner Ladies'

13 – The Founding Fifties – The Decade of 'Firsts'

'Under the spreading chestnut tree' – *girls of the founder intake*

With overseas expeditions and trips increasing, so did cultural exchanges and for the *first* time nineteen pupils from France, Austria and West Germany spent two weeks enjoying the hospitality of pupils and their parents at the end of the summer term.

By September 1957 the school had expanded to its predetermined capacity, 630 pupils, and this was only with five years in occupation and with no sixth form yet formed. Future overcrowding loomed!

The frugal times were still being felt when it was apparent that equipment was still in short supply. One Science master borrowed a reel of cotton from the domestic science department for use in an experiment and when he had used it he insisted on tying all the short pieces together and returning it – carried through the school by a winding procession of pupils!

Since the official opening of the school, much energy had been put into supporting the charity – 'Save the Children Charity Fund' – whose patron was the Countess Mountbatten. Janet Perkins and Brian Debenham, travelled to London to represent the school and present the Countess with a cheque for 50 guineas, all monies donated by pupils. This practice continued for a number of years during her lifetime, and the charity continued to receive the school's support well after her death.

Sport and outdoor activities continued apace in 1958, a second boat – the 'Mary O' – was built and launched, and John Greasley became the *first* pupil to win a national sports title – winning the boys intermediate javelin at the All England Schools Championships. He was to achieve a hat trick of wins by 1960.

In Music Janet Eggleden became the *first* pupil to get a place in the National Youth Orchestra, an accomplished clarinettist by then, she went onto much higher levels after leaving school.

In July 1958, the founder intake, now ending their fifth year sat the *first* 'O' Level examinations to be taken in the school. Marigold Hunter scored 98% in Geography, the highest mark in the country. Whilst pupils toiled with their exams, the staff brushed up on their badminton skills!

Later in September 1958 the school's *first* ever sixth form was established, 36 pupils, almost half of the founding intake, remaining on at school. The *first* prefects were appointed from within their ranks, going on in their second year, as they became the upper sixth, to become senior prefects with the appointment of Janet Perkins and Brian Debenham as the school's *first* head girl and head boy.

Nicholas Wyndow gained the distinction of becoming the *first* pupil to sit and pass an 'A' Level exam, in maths, in July 1959, scoring high marks after only one year's tuition. In 1960 he excelled similarly at Scholarship Level.

In 1959, the second intake, who had started in 1954 formed the lower sixth, with a selected few becoming 'junior' prefects. The school had come of age – a span covering seven years of pupils meant that at last the school was full.

With the award of the *first* full school sports colours to seven pupils, and 'A' levels being taken by the remaining Upper Sixth pupils in June 1960, the full cycle of development in the school's short history had taken place. The first seven years ended in July as the majority of those remaining from the founding intake departed to launch themselves on future careers via Universities, Colleges and cadetships at RMA Sandhurst and the RAF College Cranwell. Their departure was heralded at the *first* ever school fete held in July amidst bright sunny weather and opened by comedian Stanley Unwin. Over £1,300 was raised. Goodwill messages were received from stars of stage and screen Peter Sellars, Harry Secombe and Dirk Bogarde.

Later that evening a Grand Ball was held, tickets costing 10/6d each. A great time was enjoyed by all before the founding pioneers went their separate merry ways, some never to meet again until 43 years later at the Golden Jubilee Reunion in 2003.

The school had turned a full circle; it was the end of an era and decade.

A bevy of beauty - the Folk Dance Team enjoy a County Competition Win

14

THE SIXTIES – CHANGES LOOM AHEAD

By September 1960 the school was now more than fully complemented, being originally built to accommodate around 630 pupils it was now approaching a total of 900 and this without any increase in teaching space, meant that some serious managerial consideration was needed

The original principle that every member of staff taught in their own classroom had been abandoned in the attempt to fit smaller sets into smaller rooms. Pupils even found themselves building several additional rooms to accommodate the ever increasing classes. Affectionately known as the 'Palazzo del Te', the cardboard shack they built was erected in the main entrance hall. In addition, rooms were extended, and the spacious landings reclaimed to provide a classroom for twelve, cupboards, an art room and a tuck shop. With Harvey Road School having long since vacated their four rooms, ironically it became reverse order, Rickmansworth Grammar School become lodgers in two classrooms in the new block at their school half a mile down Watford Road. What a change in fortunes over the past seven years!

By 1962 a new science block was built close to the existing one, although not without problems, there had been a combination of local objections to the three storey complex together with problems over the foundations, both combining to cause a year's delay in the completion of the project. However when opened it provided a laboratory, two demonstration rooms, two classrooms, two dining rooms and a kitchen able to provide 400 meals.

Later, and funded by parents, a new sports pavilion was put in place close to the sports fields. Besides its primary use for sport, for obvious reasons, it was able to double up by providing enough space for three extra teaching areas and the critical shortage of space was exemplified when the original dining rooms, and the entrance hall to the gymnasium, were also used for teaching space.

Education, albeit in cramped conditions, continued whilst extramural interests were actively encouraged. The India Cup, instigated and presented by the school's first Chairman of the Governors, Colonel Goad, having first been won by founder pupil Bob Jobbins, was awarded successively in the early sixties to D Walker, G Stone and jointly to James Davis and Robert Moss. The award was presented annually to the pupil who showed the most initiative in travel, and Walker travelled over three thousand miles in six weeks, through France, Belgium, Germany, Austria, Yugoslavia and Italy – all this on £25.

That same year, 1962, the school's first Patron, Countess Mountbatten of Burma, passed away, six years after officially opening the school. The Hon. Lady Bowes-Lyon assumed the appointment of Patron in her place. Four pupils were selected for VSO (Voluntary Service Organisation) work overseas – Christine Murray (Nyasaland), C. Olney (Northern India), G Stone (Gilbert and Ellis Islands) and D Walker (Sarawak). This was a forerunner to further involvement by pupils in VSO schemes in future years.

In 1963 the annual summer fete, held on a bright sunny June day, was a mammoth occasion when 1,000 barbequed sausages were sold. £1,260 was raised in all.

The next year the tenth anniversary of the occupation of the school site at Scots Hill was celebrated being attended by the school's Patron, Lady Bowes-Lyon, and the former County Education Officer, Sir John Newson. During the speeches, pupil Lynne Richardson offered a vote of thanks to the distinguished guests and P. Dawson presented a cheque for 250 guineas to Lady Bowes-Lyon in respect of the Save the Children Fund. This traditional presentation had become an annual event at the school, and countless, and very much needed thousands of pounds have been raised for this very worthwhile charity ever since.

Extra mural activities remained a dominant feature of the school, and by 1964 sixteen different school societies – covering the arts, sport, drama, music, studies and outdoor activities – had been formed, to name but a few. They were well supported by both staff and pupils.

Signs of changing times were creeping in with the introduction of audio French lessons conducted through a pilot scheme promoted by the BBC. A forerunner to the electronic world! It proved very effective in the coming years.

Overcrowding of classrooms now meant that the 'personal touch' had been lost – the end of term competition for the tidiest classroom bad been discarded. Staff also now had the option of lunching with pupils either in the dining halls or in the staff room.

Pupil Richard Stone was awarded an 'Open Exhibition' at Oxford, and to the delight of everyone the whole school was given a half-day holiday in honour of his achievement.

The major 'coup' of 1964 was the successful bid by the county council at the auction of the adjacent and vacant Victorian mansion, Scots Hill Court. Situated at the top of Scots Hill, it became the new arts and music block, and provided much needed relief to the existing overcrowding problems. However tragedy stuck in 1969 when on one Saturday night a fault in one of the pottery kilns triggered a fire that completely destroyed the house. Temporary arrangements were put in place – the county council provided some old portacabins which were to house the art department, for another unimaginable twenty five years, their interpretation of the word 'temporary' was questionable! The music department was transferred to the nearby All Saints Church Hall. Expectations of new premises being found, or preferably built, were soon dispelled, the insurance settlement only provided £27,000, totally insufficient for both departments – instead enough only for a new music department.

Scots Hill Court

During the following five years at Scots Hill Court, art teacher, Laurie Primmer, published his widely read book "Pottery made Simple". It became another addition to the ever expanding Library, where the 'Canterbury Tales' mural, having been painted by 1956 intake pupil Julia Papps, saw an increase in books, numbering only 1,661 in 1958 to well over 6,500 by the middle of the sixties. As a vital part of the school it has continued to be well visited and used.
.

An 'alarming' headline and report that had first appeared in the Watford Observer in October 1964 – 'End of the Grammar School', provided the basis of the following report

14 – The Sixties – Changes Loom Ahead

by the Headmaster to the School Governors in early 1965, to quote:-

> *"At the last meeting but one, the headmaster was asked to inform governors in advance of difficulties over staffing, so that they could act, instead of being told what action had been taken. Such a situation has now arisen, and the staff also are anxious that the governors should know of this.*
>
> *The staff, as a whole, were extremely disturbed to read in the local press of "Secondary Schools for All" (for pupils aged 12 to 16) followed by sixth form colleges for those who wished to stay from 16 to 18. Not one member of the staff of this school had even heard of this plan before it appeared in the press and had been distributed to county councillors etc.*
>
> *Grammar School staffs were invited to a meeting in Hatfield, one evening in October, with the Hertfordshire branch of the National Union of Teachers (N.U.T.), to discuss the plan which they had evolved. 28 members of the staff of this school went to the meeting, which was attended by over 400 Grammar School masters and mistresses. It soon became very clear that grammar school staffs as a whole were diametrically opposed to these ideas.*
>
> *Hertfordshire heads of grammar schools have also discussed the N.U.T. plan, and are positive that such a plan would result in the lowering of academic standards in Hertfordshire, and this in its turn would mean fewer Hertfordshire pupils gaining university places.*
>
> *Many staff have said that rather than work in one of the new "Secondary Schools for All", they would seek employment in Middlesex, London or Bucks. – or move elsewhere. Once they had left it would be difficult to replace them by staff of equal quality, especially when it became generally known that there was a possibility of*

Pupils conception of school life

Hertfordshire "going comprehensive" – whatever form of comprehensiveness was adopted. Two members of the staff have already acted, and one is, in view of his qualifications, likely to be offered the post elsewhere for which he has applied".

Was this the first indication of the 'winds of change' in the concept of secondary school and comprehensive education – to be felt to full effect no less than five years later at Rickmansworth?

Outside activities continued as usual in 1965, the lower sixth attending 'en bloc' a General Studies Conference – discussion focussing on 'Freedom and Society', following up a year later with a three day conference covering 'Trends in Modern Culture'. Two further sixth form conferences followed in 1968 and 1969 – continuing this popular trend – subjects being 'Complacent Society' and 'Brave the New World'.

'Social Science' work in the community was instigated in 1966, with pupils helping in local hospitals. This trend was to continue for a number of years.

School Fete programme

On a lighter note, during the late sixties four members of the upper sixth played table soccer non-stop for 51 hours in aid of the 'Save the Children Fund', thus beating the record of 50 hours previously held by Peterborough. Mark Taylor and Dave Bourne represented 'Luton Town', local soccer rivals to 'Watford FC', who in turn were played by Michael Smith and Peter Kyre. The result was a win (conveniently) for Watford 325 goals to 313, with Smith netting 230 of Watford's total. Throughout the vigil, teachers – Messrs Adams, Goodman, Harby and Palmer acted as timekeepers, and a sizeable sum was raised for the charity.

And so the decade ended with the first, and dramatic, change in status – that of comprehensive schooling and the loss of grammar school status – being imposed on the school. As described elsewhere, this was to have a major effect on the school, and to have its greatest impact in the Seventies.

15

THE SEVENTIES – REFORMS NOW BITE DEEP

In January 1970 founder teacher Graham Heddle was appointed Deputy Headmaster whilst another founder – Peter Stowe – left to assume his own headship at Riversmead School, Cheshunt. It was an honour that he became the third founder member of staff, in only seventeen years, to go on to a headship, his predecessors being Tom Davis and Peter Rowland.

National unrest precipitated from the Headquarters of the National Union of Teachers (NUT) had its effect when 21 members of staff were called upon to withdraw their services, however well conducted 'in house' consultations prevented any action being taken.

The parents' guild accepted a staff suggestion that their next fund-raising objective should be the funding for a heated school swimming pool – another suggestion with a happy ending! The guild were fast becoming an influential entity in school life, as is described in a later chapter.

During 1970 successful visits to and from thirteen local junior schools took place – all achieving a good working relationship between themselves and Rickmansworth, with each being a local 'feeder' school into secondary education.

Late in the year the governors of the school viewed the newly installed and well used language laboratory, where pupils listen to questions on individual tapes, and duly record their answers on that tape – in the language on the tape – thus confirming the benefits of this joint county/school guild initiative in first promoting the venture.

By 1971 vital improvements to some of the school's buildings – estimated at a cost of £109,000 – were being put forward. Such critical areas included an extension to the staff room – originally designed for 36 members, now holding 67 in cramped conditions – extensions to the administration offices and various departmental classroom additions and extensions.

In fact, they were more than extensions, a new science block containing three new laboratories, with three preparation rooms, coving Chemistry, Physics and Biology were planned. In addition three new classrooms were included in the plans and as it became more of an 'engineering block', other such subjects/pastimes to be catered for included woodwork, metalcraft, engineering drawing and science, jewellery making and boat/canoe building. The total cost, including the planned swimming pool, was in fact £160,000, with the Parents Guild raising £17,000 and the county providing £5,000. Planned completion for all work was scheduled for January 1979 – and this was met!

It was noticed that county statistics recorded that the school premises accommodated 800 pupils, a far cry from the 1,020 present at the beginning of 1971. This miscalculation aside, the effects of being a comprehensive school were being felt, effectively designated as a 'five class entry' school, every year Rickmansworth was taking in six classes, but at a maximum of 30 pupils each. Classes were not 'streamed', though 'high flyers' were not put in with pupils needing extra help. Class order lists did not exist; pupils were not promoted or demoted, and remained within their class throughout their five to seven years at school. In their first two years all pupils followed a common course. Comprehensive schooling was hitting hard.

As part of the system new staff would usually take a first year class on joining and remain with it for five, or even seven, years. Careers staff, totalling thirteen by the middle of the seventies, were available to all pupils, with introductory talks beginning at fourth year. Later on in the fifth form Herts County Careers Officers also became involved in the future careers monitoring of pupils.

To qualify for the sixth form a pupil needed a minimum of four 'O' Levels, taking an 'A' level course of three subjects. By then there were fifty-one different combinations of 'A' level subjects on offer.

The school had settled into its new status, rather overcrowded and in need of much. Hugh Forsyth's overview, as recorded in another chapter, gives a solid impression of this mid to late seventies era.

In late 1973 the county had provided temporary classrooms to combat the overcrowding by way of a double size room for art, and two singles for extra classes who joined during September that year. They were turned out not as temporary as they seemed and remained to quote "well used and satisfactory in almost all respects" for many more years.

And so by 1974 the school was fully comprehensive, but only up to fifth year. Peter Morrill and Millie Collings finally retired after twenty years of joint headship, leaving the school to be steered by the capable hands of Hugh Forsyth and Marika Sargint (nee Edwards).

That year Mr. Goodman made good use of the 'Stock Exchange Finance Game', as devised partly by fellow teacher Mrs. Noble, and designed to simulate real life situations that provoke lively discussion. It proved very popular in the sixth form and was incorporated in part of their economics course.

By the end of 1977, two major fundraising efforts were in place; one a bazaar to raise money for the Prince of Wales Silver Jubilee Appeal; and two, a charity football match between sixth form boys and girls in aid of 'Save the Children Fund'. Neither financial or other 'result' is known!

January 1978 began with a bang – not literally thankfully in this case – the school had to close down, having only just re-opened, because of problems with the heating system. Much of the term saw engineers overhauling and modifying the system where necessary – the resultant improvement was graded 'remarkable'! Whilst elsewhere the majority of schools had to close due to lack of oil resultant from the 'international oil crisis', the good foresight of the school's caretaker had made sure that sufficient stocks were in place to see the school survive without too much anxiety.

Mrs. Parfett, the school's first bursar, in place even before the Scots Hill site was occupied in 1954, retired. She had transferred from Clarendon School with the founding intake of 1953. Her reputation, humour, reliability and support were deemed second to none, and her successor, Mrs. Reeves, carried on with the same light and tradition.

By the summer of '78 the lost property store was bursting at the seams – watches, pens, spectacles, socks, shorts and much more lined the shelves. The problem of providing adequate secure lockers had long been on the agenda, now it was physically highlighted – eventually to be rectified. A call went out to parents to try and ensure that all their off-springs' possessions were clearly marked with their names.

15 – The Seventies – Reforms Now Bite Deep

By the end of the year, the magnificent Christmas decorations – surpassing anything ever displayed before – needed eight boxes each measuring the size of a double wardrobe to restore everything. With overcrowding problems prevalent, there was no room to stack and store these boxes long term, and an appeal went out for parent help. After a year had passed however there had been no response. They still remained in the school, and in the way!

The continuing year-long oil crisis nearly caused closure due to now dwindling reserve stocks – not helped by a particularly harsh period of bad weather. Outdoor activities were severely restricted, resulting in an increase in time spent by pupils inside the buildings. To save on half an hours heating, an appeal went out to parents to stop their off-spring arriving at school before 08.30 am – even in many cases before 08.00 a.m. The school was unable to provide any supervision, or heat, before 08.30. (As the author, readers may like to note my comment under 'special memories' concerning "pupil authority" in the anecdotes chapter. It stopped early arrivals in those days!)

By July '79 some fair criticism was laid at parents' feet. Quite a few pupils were failing their 'O' levels, when CSE's would have been more appropriate to the pupils ability. It seemed that some parents were neglecting the fact that the school was now an 'All Ability' school, catering for all degrees of education ability, and the pushing of a pupil who was not of the right ability was deemed, quite correctly, to be detrimental to their confidence. Children of all abilities, as now admitted to the school, should eventually find their level – it is not selected for them.

The same month marked the official beginning of the computer age at the school, with the instillation of a computer terminal linked by a GPO line to the new computer at Hatfield Polytechnic, and once again provided by the school guild. It was noted however that the new computer cupboard was more popular amongst sixth formers than the very own common room. What was the secret?

July also saw the School Guild's Silver Jubilee Fete, on the 14th to be precise, organised to commemorate the 25 years of occupation of the premises at Scots Hill, and with the aim to raise £7,000 in order to provide those much needed secure lockers for pupils. It was a case of 'mission accomplished'. Lockers were installed. Patricia, Countess Mountbatten, in her role as the school's patron, regrettably had to decline her invitation, but instead was able to attend a Silver Jubilee Open Day later in the year on 16th November.

By September – an unusually mild month weather wise – the school was instructed to survive for the future on the now compulsory fixed monthly quotas of heating oil – economy was the call of the day.

As was to be expected as the decade grew to a close, the old grammar school system of distinction between classes, and awarding of gradings, and class places had completely disappeared, classes were now randomly mixed and that not in any particular order.

With the school about to pass on from one decade to yet another, an overview of the premises by helicopter would show the enormous structural changes of the first 25 years. Additions included the new dining hall blocks, sixth form and craft buildings, the science building, the music block and the swimming pool. Dismay would also creep over faces at the deterioration of the neat lawns – laid in 1954 – scarred by muddy tracks caused by 'short cutting', outside the entrance churned by the tyres of cars. That special respect felt in the fifties had been worn down by the social changes and attitudes of the sixties and seventies, particularly for 'others' property – the school had fallen into this category. A reflection by David Drew, one of the founder teachers in 1954 sums up the mood, to quote:

> "The school hasn't changed only in its buildings and its grass. It has been reorganised. I have never seen it claimed that a grammar school was improved by making it comprehensive and this school has had its share of problems since change began in 1969. Increased size, a wider range of ability to cope with, and all the organisational difficulties that that implies, have had a profound effect on the school and the tranquil first fifteen years have been followed by less easy times. The raising of the school leaving age has added to these problems, bringing that well-recognised phenomenon, the reluctant fifth-former. It is a tribute to the staff as a whole and to the vast majority of pupils that the school is coping so well with its new role. It's a noisier place, a busier place, a less easy place to work in. But there are hundred of nice kids in it. That's one thing that hasn't changed".

And so the decade ended, heralding the arrival of the eighties, a new government, and unprecedented changes that were brought about.

16

THE EIGHTIES – SETTLED TIMES THEN MORE CHANGE

And what better way to greet the eighties at Rickmansworth School than the following headline and report in a local newspaper – published on 7th January 1980

AFTER GREAT CHANGES, LOOKING FORWARD TO 50.

Rickmansworth School reaches its Silver Jubilee. In 1979, Rickmansworth School reached its Silver Jubilee with a certain nostalgia combined with a proud record of Academic achievement. However, while 25 years may not be long in terms of an Eton or Harrow, few older schools will have seen more change during their first 25 years. Officially opened in 1956 by the late Countess Mountbatten, the county council expected Rickmansworth Grammar School – at is was then called – to be co-educational with 540 girls and boys and 30 teaching staff. Such was the popularity of 'Ricky Grammar' that, by September 1964 there were 906 pupils and 52 staff. Extra classrooms and laboratories – and a second kitchen – had been added and the planners were regretting not buying land adjoining the school which had been developed as private houses. By September 1974 there were 1119 pupils, 83 teaching staff and 32 non-teaching staff in the same buildings! Today there are 1013 pupils and they no longer have to hold classes in the corridors and cloakrooms – although there are still accommodation problems which looks as though they will be around for sometime due to the present economy

Abandonment. *The second major change after numbers which one foresaw was in 1964, when selective education was abandoned, and the school lost its 'grammar' title in 1969. Ten years later, by 1979, the re-organisation is complete and almost a generation and a half of those 'all-ability' children has passed through the School. At this milestone in its life, how successful have the first 25 years been? And how does one evaluate the degree of success of a school*

Examinations. *You can look at examination results of those who leave and Rickmansworth School has a fine record. Approximately fifty places each year are gained at universities and polytechnics to read for Honours Degrees. But academic results depend at least as much upon the 'quality' of the child entrants as upon the skill of the staff and, in both, the School has been very fortunate.*

Success. *Most schools hope to encourage and develop desirable personal qualities in the pupils, but how can you measure success in these areas? Perhaps one feature which is apparent to those who know the school is an indication of its success. The fact that it is a happy school, as is demonstrated by the many ex-pupils and staff who revisit and demonstrate their pleasurable nostalgia. But an acid test of success must surely be the demand for places at a school, and each year there continues to be many more applications than available places.*

Parents. *In addition to the staff, Rickmansworth School has benefited greatly from first-class parents. The parent's guild has raised a large sum over the years to provide extra facilities, such as an indoor heated pool, two minibuses and a grand piano. Then there have been many smaller items but most recently, for the Silver Jubilee year, there were 1,000 brand new steel lockers at a cost of more than £7,000. Half this last sum was raised at a fete held last July and the balance has* *been met by individual parent donations. In view of the unexpected changes of the last 25 years, it would be foolish to even try to predict what the next 25 will bring. One thing is certain however. The school is going to continue to need the real support of the Rickmansworth and Croxley Green communities if success is to be maintained with the proposed cuts in educational spending. Both local and parliamentary representatives must be made continually aware that it is the community's wish that the high standards of education provided by Rickmansworth School and similar schools is not negatively affected by unnecessary reductions in staffing and equipment.*

In the ever changing world, maintenance of standards is still of paramount importance. Standard of pupils dress and punctuality were continually questioned throughout the decade, discipline had changed since the austere post war years, and the relaxing effects of the sixties and seventies trends had found their way into school life. Constant reminders were passed onto parents to help. Unlike many schools Rickmansworth maintained standard regulation uniform for all to wear. Teacher pupil numbers had levelled out and the likelihood of cuts in public spending as early as 1980 had a knock on effect to the extent that a possible reduction in the staff quota could lead to the inevitability of larger classes as a result.

School lunches went up from 35p to 55p, in two short stages. Inflation was rearing its ugly head. The administrative burden of adopting a 'pay as you eat' policy was quickly felt.

Further constraints in spending forced the school to request parent contributions towards keeping the swimming pool heating system going. Closure would have been the other option.

The early eighties saw cost cutting affect other areas too – music tuition was hit by a High Court ruling against charging 'music fees' – and cuts in the number of county road safety officers who ran the National Cycling Proficiency courses led to an appeal to parents to volunteer for training as instructors. The prerequisite that those pupils who wanted to cycle to school had to pass this test still remained. The appeal worked and by December 1983 training was completed and on time too.

In January 1982 building work started on both the new offices and careers suite, funded jointly by the parent's guild and county council. At the same time former pupil Nick Stringer won his first full England rugby cap in the International against the visiting Australian team, whilst is was sadly reported some months later that two other former pupils, Richard Nunn (Lieutenant, Royal Marines) and Laurence Watts (Corporal, Royal Marines) had lost their lives in the Falklands War. An oak tree was planted and a plaque erected in their memory.

Later in the year the proposed staffing cuts were made known and subsequently implemented – resulting in the loss of five full time staff. History, Music, Maths and Needlework all suffered some effects of this. Parents were recommended to make their concerns felt with county councillors and local members of parliament.

Throughout the decade, and in keeping with the established tradition, the annual Christmas Concert continued, always popular as judged by the packed audience in the school hall every year. Their popularity was a reflection of the extremely high standards attained in both Drama and Music in the school.

On a poor note, by 1983 the standard of cycling, reportedly by older boys, had in some cases reached dangerous levels, examples included riding two to a bike, and descending

16 – The Eighties – Settled Times Then More Change

Scots Hill dangerously in groups. A warning was conveyed to parents. 'Boys will be boys' is fine for some occasions – but not these, and certainly not on Scots Hill!

The annual staff vs parents cricket and tennis matches continued, results remain unknown, probably for the best, a draw would be the most sporting outcome! One bone of contention – now very high on the agenda of the government of today – was the increasing trend of absence by pupils during term time in order to go on holiday. Virtually unheard of in early post war years, it's taken twenty or more years for real affirmative action to be considered by higher authority. School time is for learning, holiday time for pleasure!

By mid 1984 the proposal by the county council to shut down the school meals service was made public. This was all part of the government's actions to cut back spending, the cleaning service had already been hit, this time instead of privatising the service, they re-negotiated lower wages for the cleaning staff, and this at the time of the year long national miners strike!!

The same year the parent's guild had acquired a computer centre for the school. Changed times were upon everyone – out went logarithm tables, slide rules, and even mental calculations, in came the electronic age! A change for the better in some ways, a loss in others.

By July 1984 yet another staff problem hit the school – but of a different kind not seen before – the threat of industrial action by the Teachers' Union in a dispute over salaries. Action, as was taken in the summer term, caused inconvenience in various areas of school activities, including the cancellation of parents' evenings. This prompted the following official school explanation to be conveyed to all parents about the situation, itself eventually resolved, though not by any means overnight!

> *"Whatever views are held about the justice of the teachers' case we would like to make clear that the most recent experience of heads of schools endeavouring to recruit new teaching staff for the coming school year is that there is a serious shortage of applicants to teach Maths and Science subjects. Several posts in S.W. Herts schools have received no more than one or two applications from national advertisements, and these applicants have invariably proved unsuitable. The salary prospects in teaching are now unattractive to Maths and Science graduates and so they are finding employment elsewhere. It must be said that it is in your children's interests that teachers' salaries are restored to a level where they attract adequate numbers of well qualified recruits".*

By 1985 the range of 'A' level courses for lower sixth pupils had been increased to include Computer Studies, Technology, Music, Sociology, German, Photography and Law. Other local schools had collaborated with Rickmansworth over this, including Durrants, St. Clement Danes, St. Joan of Arc and Westfield. This was a far cry from the basic eight subjects first offered in 1958.

A new project began at the same time involving series of discussions between the local police and classes of pupils on a variety of subjects connected with laws, their place in society, and their enforcement. Forms one to five were all involved, and the police recorded their satisfaction at the success of the scheme – a forerunner to community policing?

Later in the year the simmering teachers' industrial dispute reared its ugly head again, still surrounding salaries and conditions of service. Though the result was both disruptive to classes, with the 'absent teachers' problem, causing some withdrawal of teachers from extra-curricular activities, it was however recorded that, to quote:

> "It is particularly satisfying to note the enormous involvement by our staff, not only in many regular events, but also in games and the clubs. This was brought to the attention of all parents, with a thank you to the staff for their efforts".

This was not always the case during the dispute in other schools.

Industrial action hit the recruitment of staff, thus adding to the long-standing problem. This was in turn compounded by the high costs of local housing making a move into the area financially unattractive. Times were difficult.

As the year wore on the crisis worsened, with further union constraints placed on the activities of teachers, including time allowed for pupils' report writing. Parents were kept informed through regular newsletters, an example of which said:-.

> "You will all be aware that we have had a term of increased action by the national teachers' organisations. One of the sanctions which they have instructed their members to carry out is to refuse to spend time outside "the school day" writing reports. A few staff have, therefore, not written reports, or have not written reports on all their pupils. Other forms of action which have affected the School this term are a total of four days strike action by N.U.T. members, one half day strike by N.A.S. /U.W.T. members, refusal to attend the second year parents' evening and the open evening for secondary transfer, the postponement of the school play, refusal to cover classes for absent colleagues, withdrawal from supervision and activities during the lunch break and from extra-curricular activities after school (a minority of staff), and refusal to attend meetings after school. Whilst outwardly it may not appear that this action is having much effect on the school, since not many pupils have lost schooling and many activities have continued, from within it is clear to us that there is an effect and, as the months roll by, it is causing us increased concern. Meetings are not taking place and development of courses is hampered at a crucial time; as more than one parents' evening is missed for a class, problems are being overlooked or left unresolved (the second year have not yet had a full-scale parents' evening); pupils and staff are becoming accustomed to different standards of supervision and involvement, and proper standards will be hard to retrieve. It is essential that this dispute is settled soon, and that we should get back to a proper working situation where we all know what is expected of us. Reference has been made in the guild newsletter enclosed to a letter sent recently by the governing body to the parties involved, including Richard Page M.P., urging them to pursue actively a speedy settlement. We ask parents to use their voices also to this end.

Hope was raised by mid 1986 with the announcement that an interim agreement had been reached, however this met with little enthusiasm from teachers (countrywide), as there would be little to improve conditions in schools. The sorry state of affairs was eventually overcome with a successful solution being reached on a national basis, and Rickmansworth School returned to 'normal' in the late eighties.

Throughout this traumatic time the school was still able to keep abreast of social changes in the outside world, with the formation of a local drug awareness and support group, and other activities weren't dampened either when in 1986 for example a Young Enterprise scheme saw the lower sixth form a company to manufacture and market teddy bears. It proved successful and they were invited to attend the European Trade Fair in Brussels in

16 – The Eighties – Settled Times Then More Change

February. The scheme was wound up however in June after a brief taste of entrepreneurial activity?

At the same time 28 of the school's young sports enthusiasts raised nearly £1,000 for 'War on Want', a charity working in the famine regions of Africa, by swimming distances from half to one mile, running ten miles or biking an undisclosed distance whilst other pupils raised a similar amount through various other activities, with donations in these cases going to the school's favourite charity – the 'Save the Children Fund'.

The deputy headmaster, Mr. Goodman achieved acclaim by winning first prize in the teachers and careers officers section of a national essay competition organised by the Times Educational Supplement and the Engineering Careers Information Service. The title of his essay was *"What do you think is the greatest challenge facing engineering today"* and was published in the Times Educational Supplement.

At the end of the year, the three remaining canteen staff, Mrs. Horne, Mrs. Brooks and Mrs. McKenzie, retired after exceptional long service at the school. Miss Silo took over, a fuller staff being recruited later. Inflation was now being felt; school meals had now reached 75p each. By mid 1987, it was decided to transform the dining rooms into a "fast food" restaurant, based very much on the 'MacDonald's' style. Gone were the tables, chairs, cold gravy and lumpy custard days!

The St. Peter's Research Trust, specialising in funding a cure for kidney disease, benefited to the tune of £500 from a fundraising swim by 40 pupils, the largest group from any school to take part,

In late 1987 the school closed suddenly for a week – a 35 year old underground hot water pipe in 'Piccadilly Circus' had burst in no less than six places. On excavation the leaks developed instantaneously into a torrent and the 'circus' was transformed into a hot bubbling underground lake with a fountain – readers who have visited the sulphur springs at Rotorua in New Zealand will understand! This caused a total shut down of the boilers and heating system. The fault was repaired quickly.

As the decade rolled on parents were being forewarned of impending education changes, due to recent legislation, requiring governing bodies of maintained schools to be reconstituted. Inevitably the main aspect of the forthcoming Education Act surrounded changes in the way schools should be governed and as expected this was to lead to another change of status for Rickmansworth School by the end of the decade. The new act decreed that the school should have five elected parent governors, each serving for four years, this becoming effective from September 1988. Before this, the requirement was for only two parent governors serving for one year at a time.

In December 1987 three lower sixth teams entered the British Junior Chamber of Commerce 'Stockpiler' competition. Each team hypothetically had to invest £50,000 in a share portfolio on the London Stock Exchange. Two of the teams reached first and third in the regional competition and tenth and nineteenth nationally out of an entry of 3,168 teams drawn from 1,280 schools. Rickmansworth was the only school with more than one team reaching the top 30! No mean achievement. Maybe the entrepreneurial teddy bear experience had paid off! By March 1988 the school was encouraging fourth year pupils to take part in the 'County Curriculum with Experience' Initiative, requiring a one-week of planned and carefully prepared experience in a work area of each pupil's choice.

Comic Relief Day, a national fund raising initiative set in February 1988 saw the school partake – red noses to be worn whether liked or not. It was also a non-uniform day – some bizarre outfits being paraded, staff and pupils alike – nearly £1,400 was raised.

In July 1988 notice was given that Durrants School would close its doors as from September 1990. This was to have an enormous effect on the future status of Rickmansworth School, as described in a later chapter, and by the end of the month two notable retirements of members of staff occurred – Mrs. Marit Sargint, Headmistress for the last fourteen years, and David Drew, Head of Modern Languages Department, a founder teacher from 1954 and staff member for 34 years. Both retired after distinguished careers.

By January 1989 a Parents Support Group had been formed under the auspices of the Head of Curriculum Support, and designed to offer assistance to parents whose children were experiencing difficulties at school. It was decided to arrange weekly informal meetings, with any parent welcome.

Another change brought about by the second Education Reform Act, published in 1988, was the restriction to be placed in April 1989 on schools with regards to charging parents for activities, books and materials. This legislation was designed to protect parents, but was expected to cause problems. Funds provided by the county had never been adequate and parent co-operation in meeting these additional costs had been invaluable. The fact that parents could no longer be charged for these 'services', and that they could only now be expected to donate purely on a voluntary basis opened the door to the reduction in benefits for pupils. The act also provided for the adoption of the National Curriculum, and this was under discussion late in 1989 prior to it being gradually phased into both maintained and some independent schools during the following ten years.

On another note, when the local council abandoned longstanding plans to put a large roundabout at the road junction outside the school's entrance, the way became clear for the development of the empty land adjacent to the school entrance, to make it tidy, attractive and provide much needed parking space. Though this plan was 'financially' linked to the subsequent proposal to become a grant-maintained school, the plans were submitted in advance during the early autumn with the hope that a successful outcome would put an end to the misuse of the land as a builders dump and lorry park. The submission was successful and implemented.

And so the eighties ended with staffing levels at full capacity, particularly pleasing in the wake of serious shortages elsewhere in the south-west Herts area. The temporary classrooms installed in 1969 were still in use, despite their rapidly deteriorating state and the continuing case for their replacement. As the next decade dawned there still remained unfinished business on one hand, but good prospects on the other!

17

THE NINETIES – RADICAL RESTRUCTURING DOMINATES

The nineties opened with the 'earth-shattering' news that the county meals service had raised the price of set meals to 90p, but as this was additionally subsidised by the county by a further 60p, the 90p paid by pupils represented a meal costing £1.50. Meat, two veg and gravy had been replaced by more delectable cuisine!

The discussions and wrangling over the change to Grant Maintained Status were resolved, and on 1st September 1990 Rickmansworth School became the 29th school in the country, and the first in the county to change to this new school status. A Governor's Annual General Meeting had been held in July to convey details of the changes to parents, and it was decided that their first priority tasks would be in the areas of improving the classrooms, laboratories and workshops. Two extra staff were to be taken on, thus effecting a small overall reduction in class sizes, and money available to heads of departments for books, stationery and teaching materials would be increased by 50%. The school's insurance cover was also overhauled, not understandably with all the changes over the three previous decades.

On another score some concern was felt over the increased use of varieties of 'white correcting fluid' for personal use and additionally graffiti on school property! The product was immediately banned, only being available from members of staff, mistakes could no longer be hidden, nor could distasteful remarks be emblazoned on school property.

The annual school Christmas Concerts still continued but with 'gusto' – almost reaching 'standing room only' proportions in 1990. After that year's concert with coffee and mince pies in the school hall, everyone adjourned to All Saints Church for a performance of Britten's 'St. Nicholas' performed by the combined senior, junior and parents choirs, and accompanying orchestra.

The effects of the new status were soon felt, with long outstanding equipment purchases and maintenance tasks being properly funded, instead of as in the past being subject to non-availability, or reduced by inadequate financing. There was also no let up in popularity to join the school – 261 applications were received for just 175 places in 1991. On another good note, two past pupils were reported having achieved first class honours degrees – Christine Hulsey in Medicine at Oxford, and Margaret Hulley in Maths at London.

During the year new projects initiated included replacement of the old school boundary fencing, a programme for redecorating rooms untouched for sixteen years, improvements in grounds and building maintenance and better training opportunities for staff. All this could now be achieved as a result of the new status of the school, with the added effects of better use being made of the school's share of the county's central expenditure.

By 1992 the bid to the government for a capital grant of £250,000 for the first stage of a new design and technology centre was approved and involved the complete redesign and refurbishment of the existing craft, design and technology block, preparatory to the addition of a new art department in the next year. The original block was built in 1968 when the school was developing into an all-ability school, and this in turn had changed the approach to teaching the subject out of all recognition.

During the summer of 1992 the question of pupil attendance and absence records was addressed, in order to make all parents aware of their offspring's 'performance' in this area.

At the same time, whilst passing the cycle proficiency test still remained a prerequisite to pupils cycling to school, the practise of wearing protective safety helmets, on the increase throughout the country, was left as an option, not a rule.

On a down note, in the summer holidays of '92 the gymnasium was damaged by a serious fire, the assumption was that it had been started deliberately. A neighbouring resident was lucky enough to see it within ten minutes and alerted the fire service. Damage was estimated at £30.000 and luckily insurance covered the necessary repairs – particularly to the flooring. Coincidental with the building of the design and technology centre, the school received a donation of two Archimedes computers from Tescos Supermarket chain. This gift was based on 8,000 Tesco vouchers having been collected and sent in by parents and pupils. The scheme was devised by a former pupil, Jenny Milner, who sold the idea to Tesco's. They then agreed to invest £4 million in the scheme. Jenny was invited to present the computers to the school at the handing over ceremony.

Along with white correcting fluid being banned from school, except that held exclusively by teachers, so chewing gum was put on the banned list too. This time there was 'none' available exclusively for members of staff! Hiding expired gooey chew under classroom chairs became 'verboten'.

In September, 1992 not only could the staff relax in the 'remodelled' staff room, but the new 'National Curriculum' yearly identities formula for each year group was introduced. For so long it had ranged successively from eleven years olds as the first year to eighteen year olds as the upper sixth. They were to be renamed starting with the eleven year olds as 'year seven', progressing to seventeen year olds of the sixth becoming the new 'year thirteen'. At Rickmansworth it was internally agreed to maintain tradition and to still refer to the lower and upper sixth by those names, only adopting the new system for the eleven to sixteen age range.

Work eventually started during the summer of '92 on the first phase of the new design and technology centre, including the art department, refurbishment of 'Piccadilly' boys and girls toilets (those in London could also do with a similar uplift!) and building of some additional administrative accommodation between the careers suite and the headmaster's room – originally planned by the county council to be carried out in 1982!

By April, 1993 more good news arrived with the approval of two more capital grants in the following financial year. One to satisfy the school's bid for £440,000 for a new art and design building to finally replace the dilapidated temporary units, and the second, a further £120,000 for roof repairs to the drama and conference building. The new art building was designated to replace the netball/tennis courts, adjacent to the design and technology building, with the courts being repositioned near the swimming pool. Two attempts were made by the contractors to ensure correct levels on the new courts, the first attempt failed – the downhill team having a distinct advantage!

The new national headache creeping in throughout the country of parents parking outside schools to await collection of pupils and causing severe traffic congestion was causing concern, not only in Rickmansworth School, but with the police. Such a practise in bygone years was unheard of.

Hot on the tail of previous capital grants, another approval for a sum of £364,000 at the end of the year was confirmed, this time for a complete rewiring of the electrical system throughout the original school buildings, no mean undertaking, but duly completed as planned in July 1995. This new electrics system either upgraded or introduced new fire

17 – The Nineties – Radical Restructuring Dominates

alarm systems, stage lighting, class bells and a new electric clock complex. The latter was an innovation for the caretaker as it replaced the old system whereby he had laboriously tramped around the school complete with ladder at the spring and autumn solstices in March and October, methodically applying the one hour British Summer Time change individually to no less than sixty five clocks. The new system programmed it automatically!

With the emphasis on closer ties with Europe foremost in many quarters, the school designated a whole week in March 1994 as 'European Week', aimed at raising awareness of neighbouring European states. Everything – assemblies, lessons and lunchtime activities, including a menu each day from a difference country – focused the school's attention on European life, languages, customs and culture. It was unfortunate that this coincided with unpopular British decisions in Athens with other European governments over 'voting rights'.

The upper sixth 'A' level class, riding on the success of a photographic exhibition of theirs held at Kodak House in 1993 were invited to exhibit work at the Royal Photographic Society's gallery in April '94. A 'fine achievement' was officially recorded. In addition, three year nine pupils – Jo Pummelle, Louise Fowles and Helen Saville – became National Fire Safety Youth Quiz Champions while representing the Rickmansworth Girl Guides Company, the first time a county team had ever won, let alone with any Ricky pupils taking part.

Photographic exploits in the Darkroom

By July '94 the new and long awaited art and design building had been completed and occupied. On 28th September it was officially opened by the Countess Mountbatten of Burma. A formal ceremony took place in front of about 1,200 staff, pupils and guests.

With the set level of only 175 pupil admissions allowed in any one year, a letter was received in July '94 from the Secretary of State for Education requiring the school to review its admissions policy. The proposal was not welcomed but the school had no option but to comply. The principle right from 1953 had been to admit pupils from all parts of south-west Herts, but with the proviso to attach 'importance to the applicants family links' with the school, and to safeguard academic standards, however this had never been met with universal approval at higher level.

In February 1995 the school was 'honoured' by a team of inspectors conducting a full-scale OFSTED – Education Watchdog' – inspection. Legislation in 1993 ordained that these be introduced and conducted at all schools every four years. A full report was produced with eight major key issues to be addressed, but with praise being afforded to all aspects of the school, from governors to pupils, teaching to sport, and with the untarnished reputation of the school being emphatically recorded.

Added to correcting fluid and chewing gum, the use of 'trainers and boots' as footwear at school was added to the banned list at the end of 1994. Traditions, standards and regulations would still be maintained, with only black or brown walking shoes being permitted – as had been the case since 1953. Peter Morrill would have blown a fuse at the very thought!

By 1995 after a holiday period in which contractors were able to embark upon an upgrade of fire prevention standards, certain outstanding work continued through to into term-time, causing some minor disruption, but considered more important than to risk the full effects of a fire, and the disruption and horror that could be caused.

A month later the level of girls skirts came into question – some "levels" could not even equate to a sixties mini skirt! A new directive was published!

By 1996 and due to the excellent efforts of the school guild in raising £130,000, it had become possible to go ahead with the new business studies centre development based in the old gymnasium and dining room block. The balance of £65,000 needed had been gained through the governors' success in bidding for a 'need grant' from the government. The project was completed by the middle of the year and the revamped building was named 'The Peter Morrill Centre", being opened officially in October 1996 by his son, Stephen Morrill.

By 1996 applications for admission had reached 533 for the 175 places, by 1997 it was 578, leading increasingly to 728 in 1999 for the new figure of 185 places, a meagre increase of ten.

In March 1997 the sixth form debating team represented the school at the regional competition at the European Youth Parliament Forum at Radley School. They won and were selected to compete in the National finals in York. Going one step on from this, the school had the honour of hosting the NW London European Forum in February the next year. Richard Page MP opened the event, with ten school teams taking part.

Following the tragic deaths in the summer holidays of pupil Claire Rogers (year 8) and friend Daniel Gibbs, younger brother of Helen Gibbs (also of year 8), a memorial fund was set up for Claire, and resultant from that a cherry tree was planted at a ceremony in her memory in front of the school, and a seat purchased for the school gardens.

In November 1997 a closed circuit television system with eight camera and fifty telephone stations was installed, funded from government sources. Within a week a break-in in the car park was recorded, the police taking advantage of the footage from the tape in their investigations. A local arrest was made days later.

The Annual Maintenance Grant (AMG) from the government in 1997, part of the conditions of being grant maintained, amounted to £2,535,000 an increase on previous years but £50,000 below the national inflation rate. By 1998 the AMG had increased to £2,634,000, but still below predicted needs, however careful scrutiny of expenditure became the 'call of the day'.

The merit scheme, introduced internally in September '97 for years 7 to 11 pupils, designed to recognise significant effort and achievement, had by 1998 proved its worth, with an impressive number of pupils being awarded at least one commendation and 34 pupils being awarded the 'Headmaster's Certificate' for having received commendations for each term.

In the summer of '98 the gymnasium changing rooms were refurbished – re-modelled as two uni-sex rooms – giving more 'flexibility' in their usage!

Having well and truly settled into its new-found status, news was received in December 1998 that this system would be abolished nationally a year later. Upheaval once again loomed, and as a result the governors proposed that the school should become a Foundation School under the terms of new government legislation, recognising that difficult decisions making would emerge in the coming year.

17 – The Nineties – Radical Restructuring Dominates

In the autumn term of 1998, school fund raising projects raised the sum of £4,895, 'a magnificent achievement' was documented in the records and an interesting report in the local press – The Watford Observer – in December 1998 – quoted that Rickmansworth School was graded 37th out of the 50 most improved secondary schools in England. 76% of pupils aged fifteen plus had achieved at least five GCSE's at Grades A to C in that year.

By July 1999 the Sports Council had rewarded the fine efforts of the school in sport by presenting the SPORTSMARK Award. Qualification for this required the school to demonstrate a high standard of sports provision, both within the curriculum and in extra-curricular activities, besides a high level of competitive sporting activities with other schools. Mrs. Foster and her PE department were formally congratulated for this achievement.

Inevitably in 1999 and under the new government legislation, Rickmansworth School ceased to be a Grant-Maintained School, and as of 1st September that year it became a Foundation School, the fourth and final status change – well maybe?

The previous nine years had seen considerable changes for the better. Now the LEA would play a somewhat greater role in the school's future, but by no means as large as it had prior to 1990. It was generally felt that whilst the Education Secretary had tried to convince most people that there was real extra money tied to this new system, most school budgets were down in real terms. Money did not get past the LEA – certainly this was felt at Rickmansworth – and with a shortfall in recruitment of new staff the pupil/teacher ratio became the highest for many years.

In October '99 the second OFSTED Inspection took place – though as one of the new style restricted inspections, the school having been chosen to participate in the pilot scheme for this shortened version, a high quality report was achieved, yet again and in the same term three of the original science laboratories were refurbished, funded jointly through another capital grant and school funds.

And so ended the year, the decade, the century, the millennium, all in one micro second -on 31st December 1999. A new era dawned.

School buildings in the nineties, a change from the fifties and sixties

18

THE NEW CENTURY, THE NEW MILLENNIUM – A SETTLED FUTURE TO COME?

At one second past midnight, 1st January 2000 the world lit up. Not only was it the dawn of a new decade, but also a new century and a new millennium. Rickmansworth School quite understandably was shut – it was the Christmas break. As the New Year started it was straight back to business for yet another term – the 150th in the lifespan of the school!

Proposals were soon published for the introduction of the new 'A' and 'AS' level examinations, scheduled for introduction later in the year in September. For the current lower sixth, destined to take their examinations in the summer of 2001 theirs were to be the last under the old system.

Two changes in physical education uniform were introduced for the girls (year 7) with a new yellow PE shirt, and for the boys, also year 7, a new reversible green/maroon rugby shirt, hopefully not intended to confuse the opposition with an 'all change inside out routine' at half time! These were to replace the need for two jerseys in the event of a clash of colours with the opposition.

The school's nurse, Caroline Routledge, organised a highly successful appeal, the proceeds of which were intended to stock an entire orphanage in Brazil. It was a huge success and staged through the British Airways Runners Appeal.

Praise was quite rightly given to the retiring school groundsman – George Green – who in 1993 had inherited playing fields and surrounding gardens left 'in a sorry state' having been managed for a number of years by grounds service contractors. Grass, flowers and shrubs replaced the resident weeds.

Changes were rumoured in the structure of teachers' careers with the introduction of 'performance related pay', though there still existed a national teacher recruitment crisis.

A new school trust was put in place in mid 2000. 'The Rickmansworth School Foundation', to which the school guild immediately donated £1,000, in June. Laura Harwood achieved the honour of being the one-millionth visitor to the Tate Modern Gallery in London, only 47 days after it was opened. On that count there was an average of 21,276 visitors per day.

The popularity of the school in the area continued unabated in the first three years of the new millennium with an annual average of over seven hundred applications for the one hundred and eighty five places available, and this was amplified in the last OFSTED report in which Rickmansworth School was selected as one of 112 exemplary secondary schools out of a national total of 4,700. Both factors are proof of the success that the school now enjoys.

The most significant event in 2000 was in July when Hugh Forsyth retired. In 48 years there had only been two headmasters, and Hugh had seen the school change status four times, had weathered all the associated storms, and had led from the front. The school paid due tribute to his outstanding record before his departure into semi retirement, close by in Gerrards Cross. Dr. Stephen Burton joined in September as the third headmaster, ready to continue the good work and national respect gained by the school.

The schools links with the National Westminster Bank expanded with their input into the Business Studies Courses; the language laboratory became fully functional courtesy of Mr. Griffiths and Mr Briscall and work experience was on the 'up' with the introduction of work related courses.

A further change in uniform occurred at the beginning of 2001 with the introduction, for girls, of grey uniform trousers, designed as a winter option to the kilt. Watford traders 'Trewins' themselves amongst the last of the original shops in the High Street, won the right to be the suppliers.

In 2001, application was made for 'Specialist School Status in Performing Arts'. The £55,000 needed to support the application was successfully raised and by September 2003 the bid had been approved with the granting of DfES Specialist Arts College status, with special focus on performing arts. The benefits emanating from this award, it was hoped, would include a further £150,000 capital project grant together with an annual grant of £125,000, the latter over the succeeding four years; all of this being destined for the furtherance and improvement of performing arts at the school, however that is another story.

Mrs. Christine Titus, the school Headmistress for the last thirteen years left in July, herself having weathered three changes in the school's status during her time. Due accolades were afforded to her on departure; she was succeeded by Mrs. Marija Ullman.

Fundraising activities continued at a brisk pace with contributions to the Blue Peter Show Appeal, Oxfam, Children in Need, the RNIB, Shelter and Health Unlimited (care for the Quechar Indians of the Andes, S. America), and following on, a fundraising committee was formed with specific remit to finance a new sports hall together with a second gymnasium – to be sited adjacent to the swimming pool. The existing gym could no longer cope with the near one thousand pupils – it was only designed for six hundred or so! A new school website was introduced, not surprisingly as the world now revolves around them.

The school received important acclaim in 2001 through commendations as a result of the OFSTED report which graded them as one of the country's outstanding schools – honoured in March by the arrival of the 'School Achievement Award' – allowing bonuses totalling £29,000 to be paid directly to all staff. This was recognised by central government and had been achieved through regular visits by Performance Threshold Assessors who had examined and validated the schools performance management. This newly created achievement award, was distributed by the school governors amongst the staff at the end of the summer term, in recognition of improved test results and as a part of their recently agreed 'Performance Related Pay' agreement. This has been achieved as a result of all the hard work of all the staff. By October the school was at last fully staffed, a long time coming but a bonus in respect of past recruitment problems, much of which surrounded the high cost of local housing and in the same month another relic of the past disappeared, the new canteen window replacement scheme saw the removal of the old rotten timber frames of bygone years!

Awards are conferred on the school

As the end of fifty years history of the school gradually approached, activities continued unabated; Her Majesty's Inspectors report on the music department was "very favourable",

18 – The New Century, The New Millennium – A Settled Future to Come?

a school's council was formed with fourteen pupils – two from each year – set to hold regular meetings with the headmaster and headmistress, the parents and won the annual tennis encounter with the staff but suffered a washout with the cricket match – even Wimbledon was similarly affected – and the Learning Skills Act of 2000 saw the appointment of 47 Regional Learning Skills Councils, but more on that in the "Centenary Book" due out in 2053!

Into 2002 the school continued to press on in a high note – good results were recorded in National tests with parents receiving 'pupil progress reports' – shades of the 'feared' fifties end of term reports! – praise being showered on the teachers for their efforts, HRH the Prince of Wales showed his appreciation for the school's efforts with the Headmaster invited to a reception at Highgrove House in commendation of schools known for the 'excellence they represent', and OFSTED reported the school in the top 5% of schools nationally.

The national recognition awards of SPORTSMARK and ARTMARK, as already conferred on the school, were both upgraded to gold status by both the Sports and Arts Councils of England.

£1,250 was raised again by pupils, this time "having to wear jeans" for the day in aid of the charity 'Jeans for Genes', a worthy effort without too much discomfort felt!

Various projects were undertaken in 2002, including work with the Gifted and Talented, Crest Awards and a European Education Project.

The previous summer examination results, once made known showed a high 98% overall pass rate at 'A' Level, 76% of entrants gaining A – C grades, and a 99% pass rate at 'AS' Level in A – G grades. The swimming pool roof was replaced in the summer break and the need for redecoration continued – this time the paint brushes working overtime internally in the school in general and externally on the business studies and PE block.

The new dance/drama studio and ICT areas were completed – with new leased computers installed with high broadband internet, donated through fundraising via parents, the School Foundation and Gift Aid Scheme, but on a down, the plans for the new eight classroom block due for erection behind the existing art and music block in 2003 received a setback with the full proposed funding not being secured, and though building had started the long lamented exit for the decaying 'mobiles' was once again stalled!

A new block now in use

The school council – teachers/pupils – continued with the two meeting each term, something that would never have been dreamt of in the fifties – but a good sign in the changed times of today's world – effective consultation at all levels is a tool of good management. Even the

Football World Cup match between England and Brazil was followed – school was temporarily halted as pupils were allowed to watch mid week the morning game on a big screen in the school hall – better than illicit absenteeism!

A pupil support programme for year seven was initiated under the guise 'playing for success' with help from local national league soccer club Watford FC.

As year 2003 dawned concerns over the shortfall in monies allocated by the county council to the year's school budget were felt – cover was insufficient for the rising national employment costs. The school was beginning to rely more heavily on 'contributions', sparking the feeling in parents that rises in their council taxes were not being justified. A case for action?

On a high note, and a little out of the ordinary, year ten pupils Nicola Akers and Alex Player reached the final stages of the 'Chef of the Year' competition, expert guidance coming from Miss Loveday, and capital work started on both a new sound recording studio, complete with a control room and three separate recording studios, and a new art technology suite.

This time it was not jeans, but red roses, on the fundraising front – £1,000 being raised through a staff versus pupils basketball match, and another £1,100 going to UNICEF and the Cairo Children's Project, and to add to the diversity of national achievements now a common part of school life, Bavesh Horgoven-Lalloo achieved silver status and Jennifer Brown was highly recommended in the 2003 Biology Olympiad Competition.

SATs results continued to see high standards attained by pupils – results coming in the top 90%. However, what achievements were being obtained by pupils, staff and management, the old problem of shortfalls in budgets reared its ugly head yet again, with a review showing funding being £100,000 below the required figure to run the school. Again reliance was put upon the foundation to meet the shortfall, without such aid one can only wonder where the school would now be.

Nearing the end of the summer term of 2003, the school held its summer sports day and annual ball in the weekend of 3rd July, followed immediately by a jazz evening on 5th July. The next weekend the Rosarians (Old Students Association) held their own 'Golden Jubilee Reunion,' in a heatwave, with 400 ex-pupils attending, including nearly a quarter of them coming from the fifties intakes and including no less than six of the original thirteen teachers. A healthy donation was made to the school guild from the proceeds of the highly successful event, destined to aid school building projects. A few wrinkles and signs of grey hair were seen, but everyone remained upright, sprightly and still proud of the school – with even a few school ties, caps and hats being aired – probably for the first time in fifty years. The term was ended with a number of celebratory events including the lower sixth performing their speech and drama festival to packed audiences – had there ever been an occasion in the past fifty years when a school performance was ever witnessed with less then a packed hall? Exam results had been the second best ever recorded in the school's history – no mean achievement after all the changes over the fifty years, and to 'cap' it all – cycle helmets were declared compulsory when cycling to and from school. Even the unheard of in the fifties – bullying – was now the subject of a schools anti bullying policy. A new age – new conceptions – how life has changed!

And so the first fifty 'golden' years of the existence of Rickmansworth School came to an end in July 2003, a far cry from what was envisaged in 1953 when their first 75 pupils donned their caps, pulled up their socks, hitched their satchels over their shoulders and trekked to Oxhey as the founders of the school. Though much has changed in that time –

18 – The New Century, The New Millennium – A Settled Future to Come?

status, size, outlook funding, management, control, one thing has not – as you drive off Scots Hill into the school's grounds, the buildings still look very much the same as they did on that September morning in 1954 when the first two intakes of 200 pupils, and the first thirteen members of staff, all reported for duty to a school, destined to last only 60 years. 50 of those have gone – soon another 50 will have passed.

Rickmansworth is a school that can pride itself in turning out a High Court Judge, Internationals in half a dozen or more different sports, Stars of stage, screen and air, Musicians of renown, Heroes in armed conflict, to name but a few – countless pupils left to attain other great heights, some even returning to the education world as Heads of other schools – not bad in the first fifty years.

As the new term started in September with the school now a fully accredited Specialist Arts College, life continued with maintenance work needed, completion of the new classroom block vital, citizenship now a new national curriculum subject and planning well in hand for the World Challenge 2004 expedition to the Ecuadorian Rain Forrest and Coast – oops, hold it right there – fifty golden years ended two months ago, sorry you will have to wait for the next edition in 2053 to find out what happened!

Finally I, as the author, was invited by the school's rugby playing headmaster, Stephen Burton, to play in the Golden Jubilee rugby match at the school in March 2004. Having never retired since I first played in 1954, in those days at Barton Way Rec and OMT, it was a dream finally realised – I actually, for the first time, played on the school fields that 50 years ago I had crawled across complete with bucket – de-stoning the surface. It took fifty years – but I finally made it – to play a game of rugby this time truly at MY SCHOOL!

19

DRAMA AND MUSIC

One of the great features that helped mould Rickmansworth School into what it has become has been the encouragement given all the way through to extra mural activities – be they sport, art, outdoor pursuits, drama, music or a multitude of other subjects. School life was not only a base for education, but also for personal development. Becoming a professor in astronomical science with no outside life makes 'Jack a dull boy'. Being that same 'Jack the lad' professor and also winning either an Olympic Gold, a Hollywood Oscar or becoming a world acclaimed trombonist proves a sound upbringing and makes 'Jack' a great guy.

Rickmansworth School started the drama and music tradition in the early fifties; it flourished then and has progressed by leaps and bounds ever since. Such excellence that was achieved was not confined only to pupils, but also, equally, by the staff. If ever in a school was there a combined effort between staff and pupils, then it was achieved at Rickmansworth in both activities. Drama was much more of an extra mural activity, born out of English lessons; music was a curriculum subject in its own right. At Rickmansworth if anyone was discovered with a talent at either one, or both, they were truly 'nobbled'.

Music was taught from the start to the founder intake at Clarendon School. By the time the Scots Hill premises were opened a dedicated music classroom had been set up, above the domestic science room, and it was here that the basis for future success was laid. The classroom was subsequently moved to the newly acquired Scots Hill House in the mid sixties, without truth in the rumour that it was because the combined booming of the drums and the screeching of the violins continually curdled the milk in the domestic science room immediately below. Local taxi drivers dubbed the house the music college. After the fire in 1969 and a period spent in temporary accommodation, music is now sited in the new art and technology block. By the end of the fifties music was no longer a 'Cinderella' subject in schools, and certainly not at Rickmansworth.

By 1956 drama also began in earnest with the then Dramatic Society entertaining 750 people over three nights with their first production – Shakespeare's 'Twelfth Night' – a monumental beginning to the drama era. Star pupil actress, Jennifer Norwood, enjoyed the distinction whilst playing the part of 'Maria' of being given the opportunity as a part of the script to slap the face of one of the teachers, none other than that of Malcolm Withers, on each of the performances.

As the society began to develop under the expert guidance of teacher Gwyn Arch, from the English department, later to become Head of English, they began to meet regularly after school once a week, with pupils reading short plays and semi acting them on stage. Progress was fast, groups began to write their own short plays, proving their worth by performing them in front of the other groups.

A major problem had evolved by the mid fifties with a serious imbalance in girl/boy participation – with girls outnumbering boys four to one. The knock on effect was felt in finding plays suitable to cater for this; however this failed as usually the balance was in reverse – one girl part to as many as three boys' parts!

With the huge surfeit of theatrically inclined girls, Gwyn Arch decided to expand drama into the musical world, thus allowing lots of chorus numbers to be included – which would then be mainly for the girls thus helping to alleviate the boy/girl imbalance. In 1959 'Tom

Memories of 'those' plays – Tom Sawyer and the smoking scene, Pygmalion and She Stoops to Conquer with Trina Goldsmith the star, and Arsenic and Old Lace – a familiar face?

Sawyer' was produced with 22 girls and ten boys in the chorus, the latter less as volunteers, more as press-ganged! Tom Sawyer was played by William Peckham and Huckleberry Finn by Christopher Hart and the big moment was when (duly in accordance with the script) they had to teach themselves to smoke! There is no account of the expression on Peter Morrill's face, who was sitting well to the fore in the audience, that is left to readers to imagine! John Spurgeon, the then Head of Music led the orchestra for this production, ably assisted by Roy Abrams, who was later to succeed him in their music departmental role. Founder pupil Janet Eggleden, who by then was a highly accomplished clarinettist and Headmistress Millie Collings on the piano (of course), featured throughout the production.

Spurred on by their success and unable to find anything else suitable for the next production, Gwyn Arch set about writing a musical himself. Having started at the school with no musical experience or qualifications he had embarked on weekly study in London, following lessons in music composition, going on to acquire an LRAM in piano teaching and a Fellowship of Trinity College. Well armed with English and Music under his belt he wrote the 'Parker Plan', with libretto by fellow English teacher Jim Owen. Easter holiday that year, 1960, to quote Messrs. Arch-Owen, was spent writing the orchestral parts.

John Spurgeon's reflections of those early years before he departed show how much had been achieved in so little time – to quote:

19 – Drama and Music

> *My first concern in music was to get instrumental performance going: Roger Elliot's Band at Clarendon was fresh in everyone's mind. Any self-respecting grammar school in those days had to have an orchestra, for which a much longer build-up is needed. All the students that I remember at all vividly are the founder members of the orchestra. Janet Eggleden supplying the part of the viola we didn't have with the lowest notes of a clarinet, her sister Carol as leading violinist. Marigold Hunter and Margaret Luetchford played cello from the start, Nick Hazle soon supporting them on double bass. Nick Wyndow (trombone) and Richard Taylor (trumpet) had to show great restraint not to swamp everything else. Peter Morrill encouraged the orchestra to accompany the hymn in assembly fairly regularly; I was careful not to inquire what any body else thought, as it was good training for the players.*
>
> *In '58 Gwyn Arch and I put on a musical based on Tom Sawyer (Hit number: "What will you give me if I let you help me paint my fence?"). I remember teaching the songs in class music lessons in order to drum up support. It was significant because it provoked Gwyn into writing "Parker Plan" to follow it, which in turn led to his whole string of musical plays for schools television. Sadly, I had moved on before the production of "Parker Plan", after only four years and half a term, to be followed by my friend Roy Abrams.*

The production of the Parker Plan in June 1960 was a huge success, and with a cast of fifty. Pupil P Cox as Peter Parker and Lynne Richardson as Mrs. Parker took the lead roles (in those distant days only girls were afforded Christian names in reports or programmes – boys qualified only for their initials!). Head of Drama, Miss Elizabeth Bennett led the production team, Head of Art Mr. B.D. Jelly created scenery and Roy Abrams secured an excellent performance from his large body of young singers and instrumentalists, some of whom displayed outstanding talent. The musical was widely reviewed in national newspapers and journals and the content considered to be a breakthrough according to the Times Educational Supplement.

Roy Abrams in turn had produced an above average school orchestra, both senior and junior, and the creaming off of potential players during music lessons had proved its worth.

With good school operas scarce, more was to be heard of the 'Parker Plan' it being formally published in 1962 by Boosey and Hawkes and was seen being performed hundreds of times worldwide – including Kenya, Australia and New Zealand, before itself becoming 'dated'. Being about 'Teddy Boys', who were very much a fifties cult, the play had lost its appeal by the late 'swinging sixties', with all the new trends that went with the new era replacing the life styles of the fifties.

A reflection on the Parker Plan by a sixth form pupil, and performer appeared in the school's Nisi Magazine, to quote:-

> *"The Parker Plan" as its name suggests, was a play concerned with the idea of one Peter Parker to save an old village forge from demolition by the Ministry of Housing, by converting it into a village hall.*
>
> *Injected with a spirit of genius lent to it by the two leading characters, Horace and Willie, played respectively by Laurence O'Garratt and Orson Joseph, the work was a masterpiece of stage craft, ingenuity, and spontaneity.*
>
> *But the vital talents of these two, once called the Rogers and Hammerstein of the*

amateur theatre, did not end merely with unmatched acting ability; indeed, it was in the capable hands of our two aged heroes that rested two of the best songs to be heard, not only in this same production, but among all the country's leading musicals today.

The golden chance to witness and enjoy the great pageantry of a glittering first night, milling with a host of the nation's celebrities and seeped in the potent glamour of the live theatre, was one which could not be, and was not, forgone. Nor pupil nor his kinsfolk did abstain. All flocked to see the most controversial play this side of Chorleywood, and were thrilled to the magnificence of this cathartic epic, penned by Mr. Brendan Owen and set to music by the infamous ex-BBC xylophonist and car owner, Mr. Amadeus Arch: no money was refunded.

The staff's own productions were not to be forgotten in this early era and many famous plays were enacted. 'Arsenic and Old Lace' with Headmistress Millie Collings as the villain (the mind boggles!), 'Who killed the Count' with John Thwaites as the detective, followed by a succession more, including 'Blithe Spirit' and 'The Happiest Days of Your Life'. A notable performance came in the production of 'Noah' with Head of Physics, Malcolm Withers, dressed as a potato sack! It had been noted that the same members of staff seemed to be in all productions – Millie Collings, Stephanie Thompson, Margaret Ship, Penny Forsyth, Ken Smith, Malcolm Withers, Alan Young, John Thwaites, Jim Scally, Pete Rowland, Betty Harry (with Mike Preston as stage manager!). Then, there is nothing new, or old, about this circumstance!

By 1963 an exception to the boy/girl imbalance had been found, and the production of the "Miracle Worker" catered admirably for twice as many girls as boys. Pupils Lynne Richardson, Jennifer Fennell and Penelope Logan were the stars, with the latter two alternating the part of the blind uncontrollable animal-like child.

By the mid sixties, with the success of the Parker Plan having focused attention on music as a major activity in the school, the Rickmansworth Grammar School Choir was founded, by none other than Gwyn Arch. There was by now much inter relationship between the English and Music departments, and often Gwyn would produce a new arrangement, have it printed off in the morning ready for a lunchtime rehearsal, with Roy Abrams taking the 'training'. The choir built up a repertoire of some fifty songs, and produced their own 'LP' record (33rpm) entitled 'Standing in the Need of Prayer'. Besides having contributed to a BBC schools programme called 'Rhythm and Melody', they performed for a twenty minute 'BBC Home Service' (now Radio Four) programme called 'Time and Tune'.

Not content with the radio in 1962 they received an invitation from ITV (ATV – Associated Television Channel), in Elstree, to contribute to six TV programmes called (ironically) 'A Box of Birds'. Fame spread and various local concerts featured the choir, in particular the Rickmansworth Society and the Watford School of Music.

Ambition had bitten deep, and with the West End now a dream, the team wrote a follow up musical, based on Charles Dickens's Great Expectations and entitled 'Our Mr. Pip'. Starring in the 1964 production were pupils James Maddon, Chris Hart. Rosemary Young, Richard Baker, Diana Fraser, Mary Warren and Christopher Brown. The boys were honoured – Christian names at last reinstated! The chorus consisted of 45 singers, and included a group of girls called 'The Ladies of Richmond', and the LP cover, produced for this musical, shows them in their finery dress in period costume, sitting on the edge, not of Richmond Park, but the school field!

19 – Drama and Music

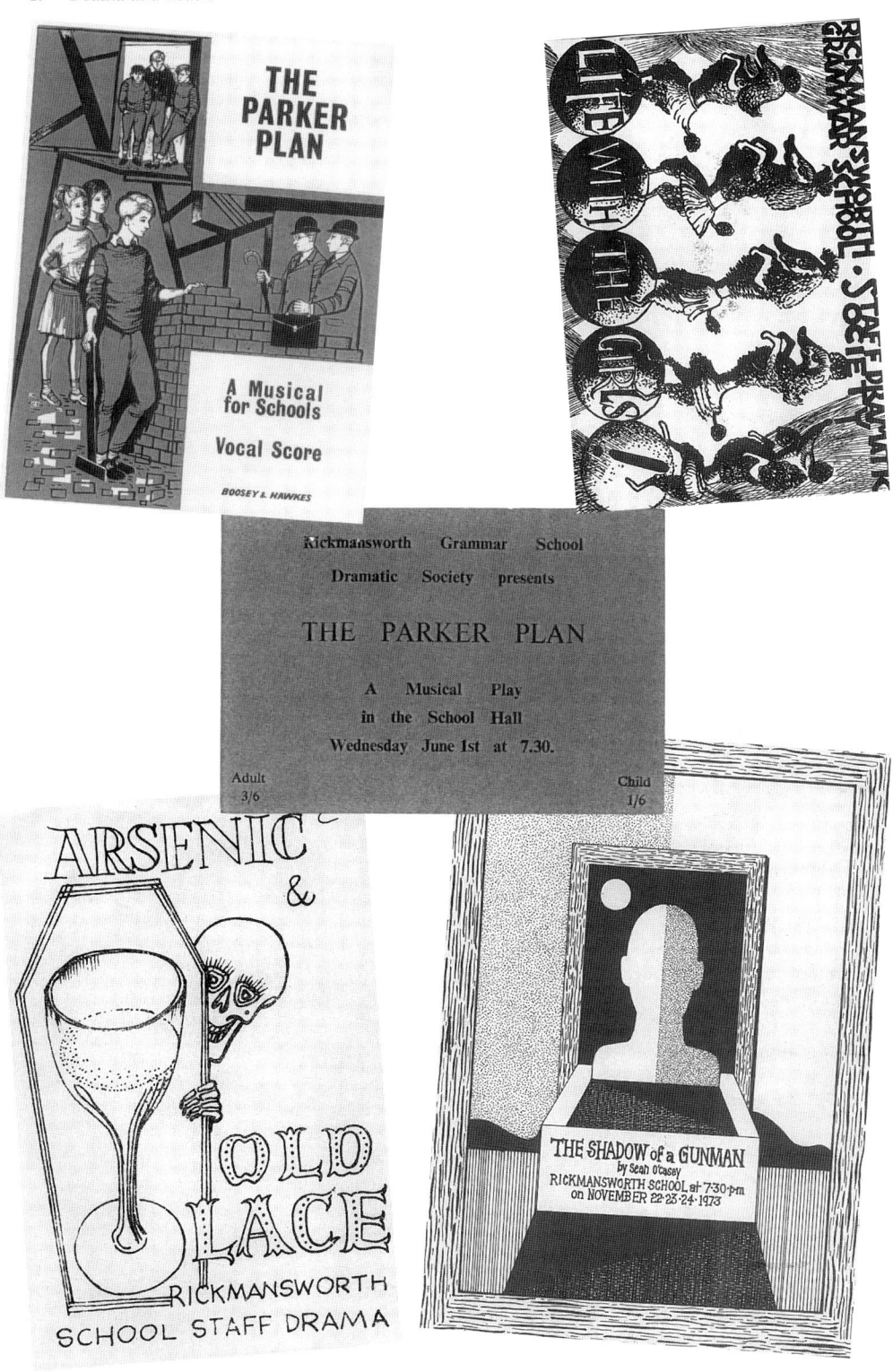

Typical programme covers

The orchestra of fourteen was conducted by Roy Abrams, music by Gwyn Arch, lyrics by Fred Tysh (a London writer), the book by James Owen and the producer Joan Lamont. The drummer, Triston Fry, borrowed from a neighbouring school, who by then was recognised as one of the top three percussion players in the country.

Despite interest from the Disney organisation and the BBC, together with newspaper acclaims that 'Our Mr. Pip' would surpass the success of the 'Parker Plan'; it has remained unpublished even to this day.

On the school's tenth anniversary in 1963 the school choir and orchestra performed Handel's 'Zadoc the Priest', and led the way to future performances in the coming years of Messiah Part 1, the whole school being involved. Mozart's Requiem, Vivaldi's Gloria, Haydn's Teresa and Nelson Masses, Beethoven's Mass in 'C' were regularly performed and in 1969 a marathon performance took place in St. Luke's Church, Watford of Bach's St. Matthew Passion, involving the complete senior, junior and parents choirs and the school orchestra. Rickmansworth Parish Church, not to be outdone were entertained to the Faure Requiem, a performance remembered by many to this day.

Noted staff celebrities included Sydney Fixman, a violin teacher and well known conductor of London orchestras and the Israel Symphony Orchestra. Jim Stobart, who became well known as Conductor of the Norfolk Symphony Orchestra, and Terry Edwards, better known for his English international basketball exploits, also started one of the boy's choirs.

The architects of this era in pioneering and establishing the music and drama activities at the school had all left by the end of the sixties, though one returned, but in a different role. John Spurgeon left in the late fifties, Gwyn Arch by 1964 and Roy Abrams in 1969 being replaced by Harvey Daguh from St. Albans, who went on to produce the school's version of Jesus Christ Superstar. It was Roy who was to return, this time from 1971 to 1983. Gwyn Arch and John Spurgeon went on to team up many years later at a new college in Reading where Gwyn became Head of Music, and John his number two!

On a meeting with Gwyn Arch recently I reminded him that I (Chris Morton) was taught English to 'O' level by him – being taken through Macbeth and translation of Chaucer's Prologue. He remembered this era of our times at the school, but emphasised that it made two good reasons to give up teaching English and turn to music. I'm not sure if he felt music had more future, or that I was so bad at both books that it forced him to rethink his whole concept of teaching English!

Memories like these from the sixties by Andrew Daykin show why teaching drama, music and school life was so enjoyable:-

> Most of my energies outside of teaching itself were around the school plays I produced – The Seventh Seal (1968) Galileo (1968) The Devils (1970). Looking back, some fairly riske choices for middle England, but Peter Morrill backed me up even when the Chairman of the Governors came to complain! In 1969 I took a party of current and former pupils to appear on the Fringe of the Edinburgh Festival – the school bought an old army lorry which I drove to Edinburgh to take all the gear – we stayed in a hall of residence but did all the cooking for the group in the church hall where we were performing the plays. We did the Seventh Seal, a social drama called "The Age of Spite" and a late night jazz and poetry (all the vogue at the time.

Whilst having dwelt at length on the early formative years of drama and music development at the school, such was its grounding that it allowed the show to go on in style, and well it did.

19 – Drama and Music

To expand on each and every play, concert or performance would require a book of its own; however readers' memories may well flood back by the mere mention of some of the other productions played to packed out audiences during those very golden fifty years of pure unadulterated entertainment. Some of the highlights of those years follow:

In the fifties, Pygmalion featured – Trina Goldsmith taking the lead as Eliza Doolittle, and she followed this with another rousing performance in She Stoops to Conquer.

By the sixties the departures of Janet Eggleden to higher places in music, including the Covent Garden Orchestra, Robert English into theatre management, including (reportedly but not confirmed) in such places as Worthing, Bromley and Canterbury and Jennifer Norwood carried on in amateur drama, and took up a career, which she follows to today, in teaching Speech and Drama, was the end of the founding era of budding starts of stage – and screen!

The aim in the sixties was to achieve three productions a year – separately covering works by the staff, the senior and the junior school. Such renditions included the staff's 'Life with the Girls', which included many of the female staff members and was reported to have caused some 'embarrassing situations', and 'An Italian Straw Hat', a colourful and amusing play.

The senior school followed previous successes in particular with 'The Diary of Anne Frank" with Rosemary Crozier, as Anne and Valerie Page and Stephen Harris starring, 'Arms and the Man' with Linda Scott, D. Madden and M. Longlands remains well to the fore and 'The Government Inspector' a comedy set in Russia featuring sound performances by P. Beard, G. Wallington, Elizabeth Grant and Barbara Lowman. Sheridan's 'The Rivals', with Hilary Leigh as Mrs. Malaprop supported by Michael Ham, Diana Fraser, John Bolton, Paul Marchant and Bruce Campbell, finishing off with the very ambitious and funny "The Seventh Seal".

The junior school equally obliged with plays, including 'Emil and the Detectives', and 'Bits and Pieces', I don't believe remotely connected with the Swinging Sixties pop group the Dave Clark Five's hit single in 1964 of the same name.

Not to be outdone the girls' choir were well received, entertained and highly successful on a tour to Denmark in 1963.

Performances of note during the seventies included the 'Messiah', a joint effort by both parents and pupils. 'Hobson's Choice' by Harold Brighorse, produced by Mrs. Tindall and Mr. Hunt which required the cast to maintain convincing northern accents throughout – with great success and J.B. Priestley's amusing 'When we are Married'.

The eighties heralded such plays as 'The Militants' by Norman Holland, 'The King and I', with 150 pupils involved and produced by Mrs. Lamont and Mr. Weever, and two other major choral works, 'West Side Story' and 'All the Kings Men'.

In 1982 the sixth form, after rehearsing during the summer holidays, put on a polished performance of 'Bell, Book and Candle' in the autumn term, a former 1958 Hollywood great that starred Kim Novak, James Stewart and Jack Lemmon.

The staff in return obliged with Alan Melville's 'Devil May Care', with another response from the sixth form through Alan Ayckbourn's 'Bedroom Farce', staff and pupils then combined in 1985 to entertain packed 'houses' to 'HMS Pinafore', with 46 performers and 88 behind the scenes hands!

Rickmansworth School – Fifty Golden Years

Two of the school's home produced LP's

19 – Drama and Music

The Orchestra visited Norway in 1985, followed by successfully entertaining a reciprocal visit by the Kychjebo School Band, repeating the process again two years later with exchange visits with Rietberg School, West Germany.

Lionel Bart's 'Oliver', again mixed staff and pupils, was followed closely on its heels by renditions of Stanier and Parkers 'The Shepherd King', and Bertolt Brecht's 'The Resistible Rise of Arturo Muro', with an outstanding cast covering age groups from thirteen to eighteen year olds. Rounding off the decade the staff resumed their individual stance after a few years break by entertaining all to 'The Ticket of Leave Man' by Tom Taylor

The nineties were heralded by an enchanting performance of 'Toad of Toad Hall', followed by 'Iolanthe' a light Gilbert and Sullivan opera that involved over one tenth of the school in one way or another.

The Orchestra undertook an Easter holiday tour to Canada, as the Senior Drama Club entered a new phase by putting on a 'One Act Plays Festival'. Later productions included 'Ring Round the Moon' by Jean Anouth, with a stirling performance by Mark Brownsell in the twin central roles of Hugo and Frederick, Sandy Wilsons 1950's musical 'The Boyfriend' and closely followed by a staff production of the mystery musical 'Something's Afoot', their first in five years.

The staff continued their new found momentum over succeeding years with 'A Funny Thing Happened on the way to the Forum', 'Anything Goes', and two one act back to back plays 'Black Comedy' and 'Dial Ten Amazing Little Boyfriends'. The senior school responded with 'Our Day Out', 'Noah's Flood' by Benjamin Britton, 'You, Me and Mrs. Jones', The Ragged Child', 'Bedroom Farce' by Alan Ayckbourn, Bugsy Malone' a popular musical play, and 'Wind in the Willows', the latter two in complete contrast to each other.

The senior orchestra, with Chris Weaver, Head of Music as the conductor and Mary Tyler as the soloist, reached the finals of the National Festival for Youth Orchestras in London in 1995, 1997 and 1998. No mean feat. In 1998 they were invited to form part of an orchestra of 3,500 players in setting a record for the world's largest orchestra. The venue was Birmingham and the conductor Sir Simon Rattle and the chosen music was Malcolm Arnold's 'Little Suite number two'.

Throughout all the years the Orchestra performed every time at the Annual Christmas Concert, and it was fitting that in 1998 they played the same music as they had in Birmingham, but this time without the other 3,450 musicians!

As the dawning of the millennium festivities receded into memory, the impetus of the last century's endeavours continued unabated. The senior orchestra took part for the eighth time in the National Music for Youth Festival, performed at the Watford Coliseum, toured Italy performing to packed audiences and continued with the annual Christmas concerts followed by the carol services in All Saints Church.

Drama entered the new millennium with a stirring performance of Jack the Ripper, Drama Comedy Sketches involving a mock paper examination reported to have the audience crying with laughter, finishing off in 2003 with an outstanding production called 'Billy' – based on the former hit 'Billy Liar'.

The Royal Masonic Girls School hosted a Public Speaking Competition in 2000, the school 'team' run by Mrs. Murray who was ably supported by pupils Laura Askew, Katherine Roby, Rebecca Ayrton, Gemma Croft, Geraldine Bayer and Kara Brooks.

An 'A' level GCSE music recital evening in 2000 produced outstanding results, guided by Mr. Weaver and Miss Massocchi pupils Eric Lee, Edward Hiller, Shanna Oakley, Vicki Hunter, Helen Davies and Richard Freeborn put on a resounding performance.

Not to be outdone by the classics, a joint staff/pupil song and drama production emulated the pop groups the Beatles and Motley Crew, drawing much acclaim from all. The jazz band performed at the re-opening ceremony of Sainsbury's in Watford and at the Golden Jubilee Summer Concert in 2002, a combined Guitar Concert, Speech and Drama Festival, sponsored by the Three Rivers District Council, covering almost all aspect of the school's drama and music retinue, and being followed late in the year by a song-dance performance with no less than 180 performers taking the stage. Result – a huge success.

And so the first fifty golden years of the school was reached with a major aspect of school life – Drama and Music still dominant – and major it was too in respect of success. From the day that 'Twelfth Night' was performed in the fifties, these departments have never looked back. Drama eventually joined Music as a curriculum subject, and no doubt from all of the 8,500 or so pupils who have attended the school there are plenty who have gone on to greater things, on stage, in concert, on TV, even in films. One ex pupil is even believed to have starred in the Channel Four TV 'Soap' Brookside! The stage had been set fifty years ago, now with Performing Arts status there should be no heights unassailable.

School bands – from the fifties to the nineties – little changes, not even the music

20

SPORT

The Fifties

For boys Rickmansworth Grammar School was designated as a rugby playing school alongside two other local schools – Merchant Taylors and Watford Grammar. Rugby, 'a game for gentlemen', was still very much part of the social order attached to life in the early fifties. Merchant Taylors were to play a prominent part in those first few sporting years at Ricky. For girls there was not the same 'social' stigma attached as there was with the rugby versus football arguments. Girls were generally streamed into hockey, netball, rounders and tennis for team sports, there were no other choices.

During the first year while at Clarendon School from '53 – '54, sport was played at a fairly low key level with only PE lessons twice weekly and an introduction to athletics in the summer term for both boys and girls, cricket and rounders being phased in separately when possible.

Sport started to take shape properly once the Scots Hill premises had been occupied though with limitations – the playing fields still resembled an overgrown minefield from the Battle of the Somme. Many Saturdays during 1954/55 were taken up by pupils progressively clearing the stones, one by one, from the fields after landscaping had eventually been completed, the fingernail and bucket brigade! The only trouble was that as many stones had appeared by the next session the following week!

The first four athletes from the school to represent the county

Barton Way Rec – it all began here

Rugby and cricket practice took place that second year on the Barton Way Recreation Fields in Croxley, only tennis, netball and indoor sports beginning in earnest at the school itself. By the third year ('55 – '56) rugby practice alternated between the William Penn Playing Fields in Mill End and Old Merchant Taylors (OMT) in Croxley, whilst girls hockey was enjoyed on the plush facilities at the Royal Masonic School for Girls in Rickmansworth. Boys hockey was not so fortunate; they practised, and played at Mill End where the facilities – changing and playing – were far from adequate.

By 1955, first, second and third year teams had been formed in rugby, cricket, girls hockey and netball and were picking up fixtures against local county schools. Cricket was now firmly established on the school field, which had to all intents and purposes been cleared of stones and tennis, netball and rounders for girls also flourished on the school premises.

By the summer of '56 cricket teams were enjoying reasonable success; and athletics was beginning to take shape with a full 440 yard grass track having been laid, encircling the perimeter of the cricket square and in the winter the first full rugby team was formed, with fixtures both at home (OMT) and away. Rugby was to continue at OMT until into the early sixties, the use of their imposing clubhouse, changing facilities and top class fields was not to be given up lightly by the rugby diehards, nor the sight of the Club Secretary's imposing black Buick Limousine returning to the clubhouse after a lunchtime outing every Wednesday!

In 1957 the first school sports day took place, albeit delayed a week due to a deluge of rain on the appointed day, on the newly laid grass track on the school field – every winner created a new school record for before then there had been none. A few boys and girls qualified to represent Watford Schools at the county championships that summer – and John Greasley went one step further representing the county at the All England Schools Championships, where he came second in the junior javelin.

By 1958 athletics was going from strength to strength with five pupils competing for the county at the All England Championships – John Greasley (javelin) – this time as winner, the school's first ever national champion – Linda Tansley (150 yards), Jackie Vuille (high jump), Chris Hill (high jump) and Roger Smith (440 yards).

In 1959 and 1960 John Greasley completed a hat-trick of wins in the javelin and in 1959 Chris Morton took sixth place in the 880 yards at the All England Schools Championships.

By the end of the decade girls netball sported five teams ranging from seniors down to U/12, with some of the future stars of the sixties already beginning to blossom. Sadly the senior team lost out on a number of fixtures due to the "consistent English weather" (surprise!) and illness amongst opponents.

Individual school sports colours were first awarded in 1957, three boys and two girls being honoured, and in 1960 full school colours were introduced – to qualify recipients had to have received colours and excelled in both a winter and summer sport. Four boys and three girls were duly honoured and awarded special ties, with the added privilege of being able to wear the full school crest in place of the 'shield' on their blazers. Those so honoured were – Trina Goldsmith, Rosalind Stephenson, Deirdre Gardner, John Greasley, Chris Morton, Brian Debenham and Mick McKinley.

The school was doubly honoured by fielding a second national champion in the fifties – Dinah Dobson becoming national junior chess champion in 1958. Chess flourished in those years under the expert guidance of Ernie Smith, one of the founder teachers, and Richard Taylor represented the full county senior team six times in the 1959/60 season.

In Cross Country Chris Morton and Tony Midson represented the county at the Southern, Midland and All England Schools' Championships in 1959 and 1960.

By 1959 basketball had become one of the school's success stories, coached expertly by Commander George Tottenham, ex Royal Canadian Navy and now a Teacher, himself a player of repute back home. The senior team came second in the county championships, with Roger Smith making the county team in 1959/60. A number of the pupils in the junior squad went on to fulfil their early promise during the sixties – with international honours coming to Brian White and Magnus Moeran who gained their full England senior caps. However of particular note was the oft times misinterpretation by some players of the basketball's definition of 'non-contact'!

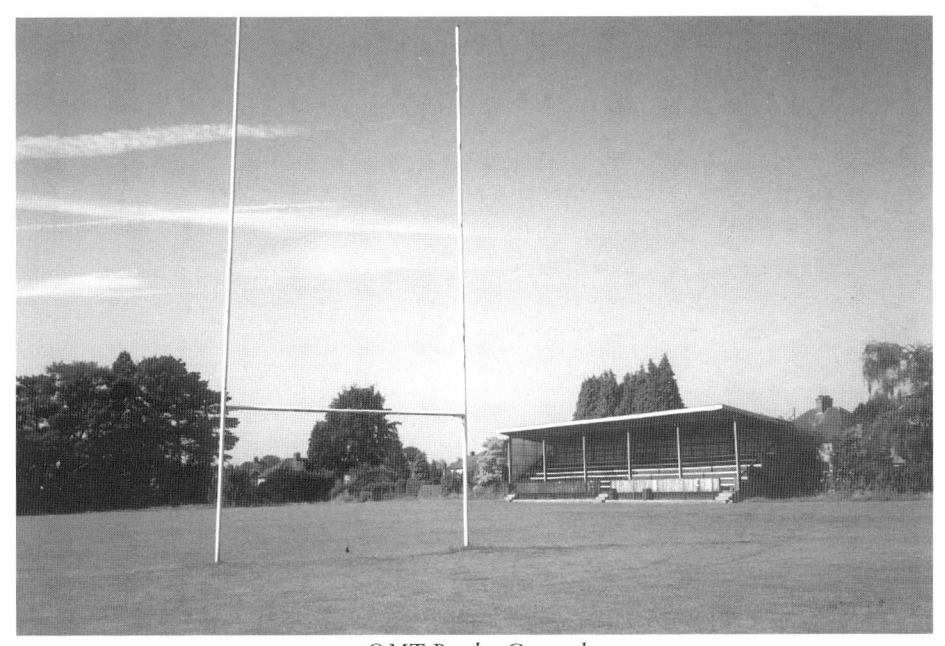

OMT Rugby Ground

With the nearest swimming pools more than two miles away, there was no competitive action, however the usual 'standards' tests were annually completed and by 1959/60 Miss

Margaret Ship, one of the teachers, had formed a twelve strong life saving squad, who met regularly one evening a week in Watford, and many pupils went on to gain instructor, bronze cross and bronze medallion awards.

Badminton, still a pastime rather than competitive sport, had kindled an interest with Keri Thompson who in later years represented both Fiji and Kenya in the mixed doubles. She was thankful to French teacher David Drew who set her on the road to success.

By 1959 the first Staff versus School 1st XV rugby match took place. The early encounters, held at the end of the season when warmer weather prevailed, a "kind gesture" to the teachers – age and cold not mixing – saw the pupils win the first encounter (just), and the whole school parading at Scots Hill and then being marched the mile and a half along the Green to the OMT ground and the privilege of the main stadium, to witness the spectacle. By 1961 these bone-crunching encounters had achieved precisely that – two teachers being hospitalised afterwards! Maybe the statement in the Sports Magazine after the previous encounter in 1960 when the school team won 5-3, that the staff would prefer to remain anonymous in the hope of being forgotten the next year, should have been followed. In the late fifties the school first fifteen enjoyed some extra expert coaching through a loan teacher Dai Lucas – himself a formidable Welsh trialist. In all, by the end of the fifties, the school could boast boys teams at most intake years in rugby, hockey, basketball, cross country, cricket and athletics and girls teams in hockey, netball, rounders, athletics and tennis. With sport playing such an important part in the school it was fitting that by 1960 the first edition of the School Sports Magazine had been produced, with sixteen pages of action packed reports on all sports activities, all years, with a host of names and performances recorded. It cost the princely sum of three pence to buy, that is about twelve pence today – a bargain for bedtime reading no less!

In the sixties John Greasley went on to represent Great Britain at athletics, in the javelin of course, and in 1963 he equalled the British national record at the White City Stadium with a throw of exactly 260 feet. Sadly injury prevented him making the 1964 Tokyo Olympics.

No account of those earlier years would be complete without a mention of the undying work and encouragement put in by the three PE teachers of the time – Barry Kenyon and his successor Alan Hall, and Stephanie Thompson. Their encouragement, organising and coaching had produced excellent results – that will always be remembered.

Typical 1st XV Rugby Match

20 – Sport

County Honours

Athletics (9)	Basketball (1)	Cross Country (2)	Rugby (2)	Chess (1)
John Greasley	Roger Smith *	Chris Morton*	C Parker	Richard Taylor
Chris Morton*		Tony Midson*	M Moeran	
Tony Midson*			(both colts)	
Chris Hill				
Roger Smith *				
Brian Hanscombe				
Linda Tansley				
Jackie Vuille				
Deidre Gardner				

In all 12 pupils won selection to county teams of whom three (*) won dual caps.

Three teams of the fifties

The Sixties

If the fifties were the pioneer years, the sixties were the consolidation years. Rugby and hockey moved from their outposts to the fresh and de-stoned green fields at Scots Hill.

In 1963 football entered the fold to rival rugby and hockey in the winters, though well behind the achievements of rugby in the decade.

International recognition increased six fold, with Magnus Moeran (58), P. Kirby and David Crump all making national age group teams in basketball, with David Crump going on to gain a senior England cap. In rugby Peter Cox (58), Derek Madden (58) and Jimmy Andrews made it into the England Schools U/15 team. Added to this a new teacher at the school, Terry Edwards, was playing regularly for the England senior basketball team, his coaching influence continuing to help the already good fortunes of the school squad in the early sixties.

Later in the decade further rugby success saw N. Smethers and A. Browsell (already South of England Captain) make it to the England U/15 trials and D. Anthony, a county player, had a trial for selection to the East versus West of England Schools game.

It was however 1966 before another national schools title was won, being the turn of Julian Danquah at the All England Schools Athletics Championships where he took the Long Jump title, only to repeat the feat a year later this time breaking the national schools record. Athletics continued to hold its own at the school, eight pupils attending the All England in 1961, this time with Girls PE Teacher, Miss Stephanie Thompson, becoming the Girls Team Manager. In 1964 M. Weston just missed the medals in the boys 440 yards – placing a close fourth, and in 1965 it was the turn of Watford to host the coveted annual event – at Woodside Stadium, Garston, itself only opened in the mid fifties but in its short lifespan having gained a high reputation, and hosted many an international athlete.

The logistics for the four days was a nightmare, much of it resting on the school's own Stephanie Thompson. Three thousand beds were needed for three nights to host the athletes and officials, every school in the SW Herts area helped. In the junior girls sprint relay Margaret Green collected a silver medal, having already achieved sixth place in the long jump.

That year the colts rugby sevens team won the county cup, as recognition finally came in boys hockey with the first county selections, J. N. Atkins and T. Hatch making it into the team.

Cross Country continued the individual traditions set in the fifties, but as then it remained that way without the necessary strength in depth to make it a strong team sport at Rickmansworth. Terry Oliver took over the mantle in 1961 and kept himself to the fore of county teams in the annual All England Schools Championships and later in the decade D Willshaw took up the reins and combined his good middle distance track abilities with cross country, and carried on the strong individual school tradition.

Gordon Adams, later to become Chief Athletics Jumps Coach for Great Britain in both the Moscow (1980) and Los Angeles (1984) Olympics, proved his worth in the long, triple and high jumps, his school triple jump mark of 42'9" remaining a record into the next decade. Both this and of course John Greasley's javelin, hammer and discus records were carried through to the seventies and beyond, as were other fifties pupils records, namely Chris Morton's 880 yards time of 1m 59.0sec and Chris Hill's high jump mark of 5'10". Such were their standard at the time.

Susan Simpson, sister of 1964 Olympic Relay Bronze Medal winner Janet Simpson, not only starred in the athletics arena, but also along with Diane Mainwood, she remained a mainstay of a successful era of netball teams. Both made county selection, and in 1966, with six school teams fielded, the 'first seven' won the county team title, Joan Elliot and Elizabeth Frewin making the county team too. The triumph was repeated in 1967 with Valerie Kempster and Linda Barnes making the county team too.

Katie Nash and Lorelei Stalford became the school's first girls county hockey team members. With hockey now instated at the school after those early years at the Royal Masonic, by 1966 three teams were being fielded and Diane Mainwood, a dual sports county cap winner, joined the Herts squad. The teams enjoyed a fair share of success in inter school games; by 1967 they fielded a strong squad who conducted a short tour to Guernsey.

The boys hockey team, always the cinderella sport to rugby, and the blossoming soccer cult in the school, had overcome their anguish of the Mill End days, and, like the girls hockey were back home on the school's fields. County caps were won during the decade by R Hill, M Barber and R Newman.

Though boys cricket kept pace, it was a quiet decade. Three boys made county schools level – P. Swan, P. Kirby and D. Barker though the girls counterpart – rounders – continued at an even less key, as did tennis and swimming. Boys soccer began its slow climb to recognition and by 1969 was fielding both a first and second eleven, thus stabbing at the very original concept of the school that it was exclusively for rugby.

The major sports of the decade, besides athletics, were basketball and rugby. With both providing the school with international and strong county recognition, team success was always knocking at the door.

No less than eight of the basketball team were selected in 1964 for the county U/18 squad who competed in the European Junior Championships in Paris, with many of them a year later making the same team in the National Schools Championships. By 1967 six member of the U/15 rugby XV were county players, having also toured Paris, and the rugby colts sevens team won the County cup. In 1969 the decade was completed by victory in the Aylesbury Sevens tournament.

As the decade drew to a close, and with the 'stars' of the earlier years having moved on, the new rugby elite of A. Brownsell, N. Smethers, already England trialists, were joined by Peter Cadle, a sprinter of quality on the track, who was making definite inroads into rugby opposition as a three-quarter with a future. They were supported in yet another strong rugby team by four more county representatives – Burton/Grive/Turner and Tanner. The rugby team moved into the seventies in strength, particularly as Cadle, Jones, Dedrick and Henderson had all made the county schools U/19 team.

The United Kingdom, a sea faring nation, has always produced sailors and ships of great note. To keep up with national tradition the Sailing Club, now possessing five boats, annually arranged no less than three sailing 'holidays' around the country, and through pupils R. Carter and M. Brown, won the National Schools Enterprise Championships in 1966, and the county trophy in 1967. In 1968 the trend continued when out of 26 entries, the school won the county 'Kershaw Enterprise Trophy'.

As so sport in the sixties had been big, surpassing even the successes of the previous decade.

County Honours

Rugby (11)	Basketball (9)	Cricket (3)	Cross Country (2)	Hockey (5)
P. Cadle *	J. Andrews	P. Swan	T. Oliver	N Atkins
D. Anthony	P. Kirby *	P. Kirby *	D. Willshaw *	T Hatch
D. Crump *	S. Barrow	D. Barker		R Hill
P. Cox **	M Moeran			M Barber
D. Madden*	D Crump *			R Newman
R. Burroughs	B Lord			
A. Brownsell	P Cox **			
N. Smethers	C Tilley			
Burton	J Madden			
Grive				
Turner				

Athletics (14)	Netball (7)	Girls Hockey (3)
P. Cox **	Susan Simpson *	Katie Nash
G Adams	Diane Mainwood *	Lorelei Stalford
D. Willshaw *	Joan Elliot	Diane Mainwood *
N. Hartburn	Elizabeth Frewin	
M. Pringle	Valerie Kempster	
M. Watson	Linda Barnes	
J. Burroughs	Susan Sellars	
P. Cadle *		
J Battle		
Susan Simpson *		
D. Madden *		
Margaret Green		
J. Danquah		
Lyn Summers		

In all 45 pupils won selection to county teams of whom 8 (*) won dual caps with Peter Cox (**) one step further winning three caps in different sports.

The Seventies

Sadly in writing this book I hit upon one snag, it happens somewhere along the line in the best of worlds, I could find very little evidence of sporting achievement in the records for this decade. Even in consultations with former pupils I drew a blank. So for this, the shortest chapter in this book, here is what little I have been able to uncover.

The first eleven boys hockey squad had a remarkably successful season in 1972, due mainly to the efforts and enthusiasm of teacher Mr Weston over the previous years and the U/16 swimming team achieved an excellent second place in the English Schools Swimming Championships in October the same year, and that before the school's swimming pool opened two years later.

Nick Stringer (in later years)

In girls netball most of the team between 1970 and 1974 remained the same, the girls having migrated 'en masse' from nearby Harvey Road School in 1969.

Girls U/16 Hockey Squad

The U/15 girl's hockey team won the Watford and District League at the end of the 1978/9 season and future rugby international, Nick Stringer, was making his presence felt on the field of play before leaving in 1979, going on to win his first full international cap in January 1982.

Competitive gymnastics began to make its mark through the auspices of the school's Czechoslovakian born PE Teacher and finally former pupils Mark Seneschall won an Oxford blue at soccer and Phillip Dedrick won eight caps for Oxfordshire at rugby.

20 – Sport

Maybe the lack of information highlights government thinking at the time that competitive sport was bad for schoolchildren in the comprehensive age – after all competitiveness had been eradicated from the education system and classroom – so why not also extend the thinking to the sports field. Maybe that's why we as a nation only one solitary bronze medal in athletics at the Montreal Olympics. I'm glad it was a short lived concept!

That's it – sorry!

The Eighties

Sport flourished in the eighties, not having been overtaken by the philosophy that competitiveness was harmful to children. International honours continued to thrive, both with pupils and now teachers.

Nick Stringer followed the athletics and basketball achievements of the sixties by winning his first of a dozen or more full England caps as a full back/wing three-quarter at rugby. That first cap on the wing was won at Twickenham in the famous England / Australia game in January 1982. Such fame was not so much accredited to the game, and England's victory, as to the half time display by a well known fan as she 'streaked' across the hallowed turf, ushered away appropriately covered by two policeman's helmets. As your author I was lucky to bear witness to that game, but not the half time entertainment, I'd sneaked out unknowingly to quench my thirst!

In 1980 PE Mistress, Miss Marshall, was selected for the England Netball team for their encounter with Scotland, and by 1981 another member of the PE Staff, Miss Morris, already a county player, made it to an England Hockey trial. Not to be outdone Mrs. Kim Lambden, another member of the staff, earned her full England Netball cap by making it into the team for the World Championships in Singapore.

In 1982 karting was made a brief appearance in the calendar with the school team gaining a second place in the county championships. Signs of modern day sport!

The exploits of the staff in netball had its knock-on effect on pupils in when 1984 Sarah Gommack (U/16) and by 1987 Alison Hawkes (U/16) and Pippa Simmons (U/16) all made it to the England Trials in their respective age groups, Pippa being selected later for the East of England Squad, followed in 1989 by another England Trial at U/19 level.

With competitive swimming and diving much on the increase, the opening of the school swimming pool in the previous decade must have had an effect on this! With the open air pool in Rickmansworth now shut, the only alternative had been the Watford Public Baths, thus both codes had not featured prominently in the school sporting circles until the school's pool opened. In 1984 Emma Batkin made it into the England Junior Diving Squad and three years later Spencer Wheeler attained fourth in the U/16 100m freestyle rankings and a place in the national squad.

Carrying on the strong individual rugby traditions Chris Goad, already an U/16 county player made it to an England schoolboy's trial.

Team sports continued, though noticeably there was only one championship honour, that in netball where in both 1988 and 1989 the school squad represented Herts in the national schools championships.

By 1982 the badminton team had joined the county league; a sport often treated more as a pastime also had its strong competitive slant. At last the school was on the badminton map too.

In athletics it was a quiet decade, both on the track, and in the field. Though a smattering of pupils made it into the county teams for the All England Schools, little success was achieved, with one exception, in 1989 Vicki Honour, already the county champion, went on to gain third place and bronze medal in the All England Schools girls javelin.

Finally, late in the decade Stephen Bunce, Mark Smithers, Mark Beveridge and Duncan Beveridge all became members of the England U/16 Swimming Squad.

County Honours

Rugby (5)
Nicholas Kemp (U/19)
Chris Goad (U/16)
Gary King *(U/16)
Ian Cooper (U/14)
Jon Bevis (U/14)
(Mr. Lambden – teacher, captain of Herts Senior Team)

Cricket (1)
Neil Sen (U/15)
(Mr. Thomas – teacher – Durham)

Football (2)
Geoffrey Hargreaves
Gary King *

Netball (10)
Claudia West (U/16)
Sarah Gommack *(U/16)
Lindsey Gommack (U/16)
Louise Donnelly (U/16)
Caroline Smethers (U/16)
Pippa Simmons *(U/16)
Alison Hawkes (U/16)
Janet Fricker (U/16)
Lisa Hale (U/16)
Sally Champion (U/18)

Girls Hockey (3)
Paula Rees (U/18)
Lisa Beare (U/16)
Alison Tooke (U/18)

Tennis (2)
Fiona Simmons
Pippa Simmons *

Athletics (4)
Alison Bone (U/17)
Sarah Gommack *(U/17)
Jacqueline Woodburn (U/15)
Vicki Honour

Cross Country (1)
Sylvia Horsely

In all 25 pupils won selection to county teams with three (*) winning dual caps.

The Nineties

The boys' strong rugby traditions of the earlier decades were in decline by the nineties, in fact they were being well and truly upstaged by the girls. Women's rugby in the country had been on the increase following the lead taken in the UK, USA, New Zealand and Holland. The England Women's team had even won the World Cup, and Rickmansworth's contribution for future success would come in the form of rising star

Girls rounders practice

20 – Sport

Suzie Cochram, by 1999 an England U/15 squad member. Not far behind was Helen Sherrif already established in the Girls U/16 Regional Team.

No boys won rugby county colours during the decade even with the services of new member of staff, David Parker, a former England international who taught from 1992 – 1998 when he retired from teaching. It was left to soccer to take the initiative fielding a strong squad including three county players – Steven Kelly, John Carter and Grant Cornoch.

Cricket nets

Over the muddy fields, in the woods and across the plains Simon Bishop notched up county cross country appearances in four consecutive years between 1992 and 1995. Paul Bishop and Matthew Barrett followed in his footsteps, and Claire Thomes flew the flag for the girls by gaining her colours two years running. Kyla Bowen la Grange ensured that the school's strong individual cross country running reputation would be carried into the new millennium, turning out for the county in 1999 and 2000.

Whilst no boys excelled in hockey, Rebecca Paddich and Anna McGoughlin won county caps in girls hockey, whilst Helen Goodfellow and Joanna Lemu did likewise in netball. The boys counterpart – basketball – once the strength of the school's sporting codes in the fifties and particularly sixties seem to have faded into oblivion, not one player reached any representative level.

In the summer the athletes were quiet, only five boys and one girl making it through the county to the National Schools Championships and it was left to Steven Kelly to put the 'icing on the cake' by finally, after 36 years, beating John Greasley's javelin record, first set in 1957. Gary Williams (pentathlon 1994) and Tara Holm (javelin 1998) both won county titles in their events to bring some credit to the sport and school.

1st XV Rugby Squad

In other disciplines the boys cricketers were steadied by their three county campaigners, Roshan Patel, Kelvin Weekes and Faiz Ahmed and swimmers Gareth Wilson, Samantha Wilson, Emily Harris and Ketty Leadbetter obtained the qualifying times necessary to gain national rankings.

The dragon boat racing team, who featured several members of the school and later Rosarians and had been a part of the local Batchworth team, represented Great Britain in 1997 at the European Championships in Germany and again in 2000 in South Africa, where they won the overall championships. These ex pupils included Michelle Smeed (70), Quentin Webb (71), Robert Crawley

Girls Hockey Team

(75), Nick Evans (67) – and his son Thomas Evens (91). Nick has been a regular member of the British team, taking in various worldwide tours.

In all the nineties were lean years compared to some of the previous decades, but at least the 'international' status was maintained – through Suzie Cochram.

County Honours

Cross Country (4)	Soccer (3)	Athletics (6)
Simon Bishop (4 years)	Steven Kelly* (U/16)	Robert Davenport (U/17)
Paul Bishop	John Carter (U/15)	Tom Phillips
Claire Thomas	Grant Cornock (U/14)	Steven Kelly*
Kyla Bowen La Grange		Craig Osborne
		Ian Houldsworth
		Tara Holmes

Cricket (3)	Girls Basketball (1)	Girls Hockey (2)
Roshan Patel	Helen Goodfellow (U/18)	Rebecca Paddich
Kelvin Weekes		Anna McGloughlin
Faiz Ahmed		

Girls Rugby (2)

Helen Sherrif (U/16 Regional)
Suzie Cochram (Regional and England U/16)

In all 20 pupils gained county colours with one (*) winning a dual cap.

And – year 2000 plus

Once the festivities had died down, the sore heads repaired, the fun over, it was back to the drawing board, with the girls rugby stealing the early limelight. No fewer than five girls – Suzie Cochram, Karina Page, Jenny Evans, Helen Sherif and Siobham Kerrigan – played for London and SE Regions teams in 2000. Rugby has changed since those early days at Barton Way, Mill End and OMT when only boys (and men) were allowed to play nationally down to school level. The reversal in fortunes by the sixth decade of the life of the school is remarkable; girls' rugby now dominated the sporting calendar, boys' rugby – shunted well down.

Kyla Bowen La Grange and Emily Harris kept the muddy footpaths and ploughed fields alive continuing with their county cross country endeavours and Anna McGloughlin, Rachel Shore and Catherine Freeman started the millennium hockey calendar off with a flourish by keeping county representation firmly on the map at Rickmansworth, all in different age groups ranging from U/21 to U/15 respectively. Anna was also picked up by the regional academy.

After so many years as rich mans game, golf had become the newest sport to offer county recognition, with Andrew Kay becoming county team captain and Louise Kay grasping it fairly and squarely when called up for the Hertfordshire team – going on to the highest level by becoming national champion with her partner.

Highlight of the year was Sarah Burrett's selection and participation at the Paralympics, held in Sydney along with the Millennium Olympic Games. She played basketball from her wheel chair, reduced mobility in her right leg being the cause. A revival of the school's one proud basketball reputation was sorely needed.

The adverse weather – rain and flooding – had its effect in 2000, but not enough to prevent Jade Hutchinson and Belise Law making the county U/18 netball squad, Jamie Rowe and David Nelmes the boys county U/14 rugby squad, the school team winning eight of their eighteen games, and the football team winning a similar number out of their 24 matches. All this achievement was rounded off by Katrina Cella being selected to represent the England Girls Gymnastics team in the Czech Republic.

And so the first year of the new millennium had again proved Rickmansworth's prowess on the sports field. 2001 was not to be outdone though, pupils Simon Roney and Steven Milligan together with teacher Mr. Seaburne won the Herts School Golf Association Team Championships and the Camelot Cup, the latter being the Three Rivers District Council Championships.

Rugby training – modern methods

The weather played havoc with summer activities in 2001, rounders and cricket suffering the most with only average seasonal performances. However the girls and boys athletics teams came second and third respectively in the District U/20 team championships, with Anna McGloughlin going on to win the county long jump title and Matthew Luddington taking third in the shot putt.

Representative honours were well spread, Danny Greave and Chris Geary were selected for training at the National Rugby League Coaching Academy, organised by Sport England whilst in Rugby's Union code both boys together with Russell Fisher and Charlie Ridley were included in the County Squad. Ashley Harris gained selection into the Great Britain U/14 World Class Swimming Programme, and at District level six girls achieved successful selection into the U/15 Netball Squad.

During August 2002 pupil Sarah Burrett toured Japan with the National Women's Wheelchair Basketball team, as earlier in the summer yet again weather played havoc with team sports, the rounders teams only managing two games and the four cricket teams getting only a total of ten matches between them. However, athletics carried on unabated with Chris West, 100 metres, Risha Rovalo, high jump, gaining silver medal spots in the County Championships as the bronze medal in the girls javelin went to Katherine Evans.

The winter of 2002/3 saw much more activity, rugby, football, hockey, netball and basketball teams all competed in district and county competitions as the year nine and the senior girls cross country team won the district championships, Emily Harris taking the individual title in first place. A number of pupils gained individual recognition with selection to county and district teams, amongst them:

Football: George Dalton, Nick Hobden, Ben Hug, Chris Johns, Adam Mitchell, Sebastian Montague and Tom Nelmes.

Rugby: James Rowe

Girls' Rugby: Natalie Adams, Cathy Adams, Kerry Clifft, Lucy Colbeck, Nicky

Dormer, Laura Evans, Emily Harris, Micki Kerrigan, Drew Kerrigan, Becky Roby, Katie Roby, Ellen Sanders, Megan Sanders and Lauren Shipperly.

Girls Hockey: Sally Arthur, Kerry Clifft and Georgina Raysbrook.

Going one better, Katrina Cella was selected for the World Class Start Programme in gymnastics and Ashley Harris again trained with the Great Britain Swimming Squad at Loughborough University.

Michaela Staniford

Girls rugby in action

To prove, if it was necessary, that the girls' rugby union squad had taken the mantle as the top team in the school, they also turned out to be the best in the land by winning the English Schools Rugby Football Union Seven-a-Side Competition at Rosslyn Park – the home of national rugby sevens. It was Friday 28th March when they won the coveted title, recording a score of 28 points to 5 over Christ's Hospital from Sussex. Five members of the aforementioned county squad plus Diobhan Kerrigan, Sian Kelly, Kayleigh Morris, Pilar Arranz-Martin, Laura Lee, Katherine Evans, Cathy Freeman and Michaela Staniford made up the victorious school squad, with Michaela being awarded the player of the tournament award. The boy's team also took part, performed well but not far enough.

The boys U/16 rugby league team reached the semi finals of the 'other' rugby code's national schools competition, losing out in a hard fought game to Hull School who had fielded an experienced team of boys who regularly played alongside the many professional rugby league academy teams. Rugby League was born in the north of England in 1893, and has remained a strongly supported game there even since. On an encouraging note Ricky's Ross McCann was voted man of the match.

In cross country Kyla Bowen la Grange gained runners up spot in the district senior race, and Emily Harris won the year ten race. Both years nine and ten won their respective team races.

Miles Edmunds and Guy Edmunds both become County Fencing Champions, progressing to the British Youth finals.

The senior hockey team reached bronze medal position in the county tournament, and the golf team of Antony Palmer and Tom Smith won the Herts Schools Golf Association Team Championships, second place also going to Rickmansworth through the pair Ross McCann and Iain Harley.

20 – Sport

Rachel Shore made it into the County U/17 Hockey team and teamed up with Cathy Freeman, Katie Roby, Megan Sanders and Louise Kay in selection for the Regional Excellence Squad.

Boys basketball re-emerged on the scene after many years, with the year eleven team joining the county league – performing with mixed fortunes.

Whilst in boys rugby two players received county recognition, one with Herts, one with Middlesex, no less than seventeen girls reached Herts U/16 squad with thirteen of them making it into the Eastern Counties squad. Going one better, Michaela Staniford, Cathy Freeman and Emily Harris were all picked for the England U/19 squad. In 2005 Michaela, having left the school the previous year, became England's youngest ever full international in the Women's Six Nations Rugby Championship, gaining her cap at Cardiff in the Wales/England encounter.

In Rugby League Tom Nelms, Chris Johns and Louis Robinson all reached the South of England and Great Britain U/14 Squads.

Other notable honours were recorded when Ashley Harris made it into the Great Britain Swimming Team, Dan Beels into the East of England Basketball Squad and Adam Collins, Rob Souter and Arran Bowen-La-Grange were selected for the County Water Polo Squad.

And so as the summer term ended, with a healthy smattering of gold, silver and bronze medal places at the district athletics championships, inter-house competitions continued – in all sports – the red, green, blue and yellow house colours all brightening the sports fields in a gloriously hot summer.

And so at the end of fifty golden years, Rickmansworth School can be proud of its endeavours, be it in the gym, on the green grass fields, through the woods and over the hills, in the water, or on the 'all weather surface' courts. To have groomed pupils to go on and become individual internationals at senior level in eight different codes, including athletics, basketball, rugby union – men and women, gymnastics, badminton, swimming, dragon boat racing and netball just about says it all! Such stars included John Greasley, Magnus Moeran, Brian White, Sarah Burrett, Nick Stringer, Michaela Staniford, Katrina Cella, Keri Thompson, Ashley Harris, Nick Evans and teachers Mrs Kim Lambden, Miss Marshall and Mr Terry Edwards. Add to this Suzie Cochram gaining an England Girls U/19 rugby union cap and the 'proof is in the pudding'. The school was born to encourage sport and competition and became one that never succumbed to 'those' who considered competition for children to be bad.

21

TRAVEL, EXPEDITIONS AND ADVENTURE

This chapter should not be compared with a high street travel shop brochure, it may have details of as many trips in it but there are no deals, costs or offers included! Instead read it as what it is – the Rickmansworth School golden travel tale.

To record every single school organised trip – at home and overseas – would require as much space as two volumes of the Encyclopaedia Britannica. Basically – it is yet another aspect of the first fifty Golden Years that has been a huge success both for academic and extra curricular reasons.

It all started, if my memory serves me right, in 1954 when one Saturday morning a crowd of us (second year by then) made our way to Watford Junction to catch the local steam hauled branch line railway train to St. Albans, for the short walk to Verulamium – the old Roman City – on which St. Albans was founded. We survived a conducted tour, and for our efforts had to write a short book about the trip and what we found. I still have mine – a little primitive, and not Booker Prize material!

The fifties were lean years in respect of the number of school trips in comparison with succeeding decades, possibly put down to a lack of finance – school and pupils – and the slow recovery of the continent after the catastrophic effects of the war on the landscape and buildings. The first recorded overseas trip, and one to set the standard for the future took place in 1956 with the Anglo/French cultural exchange trip to Caen in Normandy, Northern France. Pupils went by ferry, stayed in local houses, learned the language, and welcomed their French hosts back at home in England not long afterwards. Not long after in 1956 the first geographical orientated trip took a group of sixteen pupils to the Peak District in Derbyshire, a trekking and youth hostelling escapade, headed by two teachers and an over normal amount of rain. The sun never shone.

The first continental expedition proper took place in 1957, when twenty pupils took in Belgium, W. Germany, Austria and Italy, headed by Millie Collings and Peter Stowe, and all for £29 each. The journey covered sixteen days, staying in a mixture of youth hostels and local residents' houses. Travel was by boat, train, bus or by the soles of the feet! Amongst the more daring parts of this trip, as highlighted in the following post tour report, covers in particular the journey into Italy, to quote.

> *The holiday took place during the summer of 1957 from 26th August to 14th September. We had crossed the channel via Dover and Ostend, recollects one pupil, then on into Belgium and by train to Germany. After travelling down the Rhine Gorge, we stayed for one day at Alzey as the guests of the local schoolchildren. From there we went through Stuttgart to Ulm, and then into the Alps. We then left Germany and entered Austria and stayed at Innsbruck in the Tyrol. From there onwards we travelled mainly by foot, up the Sill Valley, over a col in the Brenner Pass into Italy. We walked along the Val de Vizze and back into Austria, down the Zillertal and back to Innsbruck. We then started the homeward journey back to England via Lake Constance and the Rhine Valley.*
>
> *There were twenty-two persons in the party, including ten boys and ten girls. Each night we stayed at a Youth Hostel, the cost of the whole holiday per person was £29. A cost at today's prices doesn't bear thinking about!*

Meeting the 'locals' on the 1957 trip to West Germany

Our Headmistress and Latin teacher, Millie Collings, led us, together with our Geography teacher, Peter Stowe. Halfway along our walk between Austria and Italy, on top of the bare windswept pass, we passed through the Italian Border Post. There was something seriously wrong as we returned because they were not letting us cross back into Austria and were becoming very excitable, and nobody in our party spoke Italian!

Miss Collings saved the day however by conversing with the customs officials – in Latin! The similarity was enough for her to learn that none of our passports bore entry stamps, and thus by some weird metaphysical logic we could not officially "depart". The solution that was agreed upon was for one of the soldiers to gather up all our passports and motorcycle all the way back to our entry post and get them officially stamped.

We lounged around for a few hours while the afternoon drifted into evening then, after the passports' reappearance, into darkness. While coming off the mountain one girl twisted her ankle on the rocky path and again an Italian soldier came to the rescue by carrying her on his back down the mountain. Were it not for Miss Collings' Latin skills, we might have landed in jail".

In 1958 a second continental trip took place, this time avoiding Italy(!) but taking in Switzerland instead. Again the group of twenty was split evenly between fourth and fifth form boys and girls, and headed by two teachers. It was a memorable trip, especially in Zernez, Switzerland where some boys, late back from a visit, somewhere in the town, entered the Youth Hostel by climbing up the drain pipes – straight into the girls dormitory! Their popularity next day was zero – I know to my cost!

21 – Travel, Expeditions and Adventure

These trips together, with another continental sojourn in 1958, this time only to Italy, had been a huge success. From then on the precedent had been set; it was not to be just one continental trip per year – but two, or three, sometimes four, and not purely for cultural or sightseeing reasons.

In the early sixties skiing trips started, becoming regular events on the calendar with two annually – one at Christmas, the other at Easter. Favoured destinations included single trips to, or a combination of such destinations as Switzerland, Austria, Italy, France and latterly Bulgaria. A typical trip included stories such as this on in 1964.

A year later, on top of Switzerland!

> *A Ski-ing Holiday to Switzerland took place during the Easter holidays; twenty-five senior pupils were involved in the trip to Gossensass, a small Swiss village close to the Italian Tyrol. Behind that rather bald statement lie some extraordinary memories: there was the passport inadvertently thrown out of the train window some twenty miles outside Innsbruck on the return journey, and the subsequent smuggling of one rather worried young lady through four countries. There was the all-night vigil with another, who found the après ski too much for her and succumbed to an asthma attack. We had to rescue the young ladies from the ski instructors – or was it the other way round? We watched with mounting horror the every-increasing pile of broken skis. However, by the way of compensation, we enjoyed the thrill of ski-ing for the first time down a real mountain; we relished the ever-changing panorama of the sun on the mountains, as we viewed it from the chairlift; and we had a holiday that none of us will ever forget.*

Tired bodies, aching feet, it's lunchtime – yippee!

And on the post trip report it was quoted that – *"there had been no major accidents"*. What were the minor ones that went unnoticed then? The mind boggles!

After the fifties annual exchange visits became commonplace and still continue, Caen and La Rochelle in France, Mainz (Robanus Maurus Gymnasium) in Germany, being the regular haunts. These were academically language orientated, however other curriculum subjects were also 'in on the act' – with annual Biology and Geography field courses, mainly around the UK, with Wales, south and north, Taunton in Somerset, the Isle of Wight and even Dorking, Surrey, featuring as popular locations.

A pupil's account of a typical Dorking trip follows – proving that project work came first, even at Juniper Hall in 'Deepest Darkest Dorking'!

> *Each year some twenty lower sixth geographers travel to Juniper Hall, near Dorking, Surrey, to take part in a one week field course. There can be few members of the school who know much about these activities, and so an account of the Dorking field course should prove interesting.*
>
> *The object of the course is not merely to learn more theoretical Geography, but to relate existing knowledge to its practical aspects. This invaluable opportunity is realised in the Juniper Hall area – predominantly chalk country with a wide variety of geological, physical, settlement, and land use features. It is accomplished by outdoor demonstrations, unaided project work in the field, and short discussions in the evenings. Parties arrive on a Wednesday, and the first two full days are devoted to walks across the surrounding countryside, when various landscape features are examined under the supervision of a member of the centre's staff. On the third day river terraces are the subject of observation, and the majority of the work involved the mapping of these features by small groups working independently. Sunday morning is left free, and there is a short expedition in the afternoon. On the following day small groups undertake projects; this involves the study of settlement or relief features in the area. The final day is devoted to a coach journey to the central Weald and the south Downs, to adjust local studies to their wider regional setting. This coach journey gives students a chance to assess the respective merits of Lewes and Brighton, and also to air the usual repertoire of songs, quite apart from the geographical aspects.*
>
> *This time it is the Dorking Field Course, which is an important opportunity for geographers. This year everyone had a good time, in many ways, and although it was not holiday it was generally conceded as "much better than school".*

Popular in later years were historical trips to the battlefields of the First World War – Flanders and the Somme becoming regular haunts, with no less than 150 pupils taking part in one trip alone in year 2000.

The continental expeditions continued, and became more advanced – self-propulsion being considered a more economic and independent way to travel. Two separate tales of an expedition through France and Spain in 1963 follow.

> *On the morning of April 23rd 1963, three mud-begrimed mini buses arrived in the forecourt of Rickmansworth Grammar School. Thus ended three weeks of proud endeavour, sterling independence, bold adventures and self-inflicted lunacy.*
>
> *Who could forget that moment of relief when, at 9.30 p.m., dinner was at last announced, and the mad charge to that quaint Spanish dining room revealed it crowded with people who had taken the precaution to get there first. Who could forget the meal we finally and disgustedly pushed aside at 10.30? Believe me, we are trying hard to.*
>
> *Surely there was a brighter side, you say brightly. Indeed, yes. The sun shone once and we sunbathed – and then we dug the vehicles out of the sand dunes; and then the number plate fell off; and there was a puncture outside the walls of Avila and everybody laughed.*
>
> *There was that evening in Pau. Our leader had selected with intuitive precision the most decadent hostelry in town. What with the bowling alley and the pin tables, there was no hope of a night's rest on the floor above, so we sang, and the French*

21 – Travel, Expeditions and Adventure

> *shouted, and we showed off by singing three parts and they applauded, so Ann Sealey demonstrated the Charleston. And that flamenco dancing in Granada! The flower-bedecked back street of Cordoba! And Mr. Stowe's ecstatic expression as he photographed the red soil, and the flood plains, and the red soil! Oh yes, it was very cultural, and even, I suppose, very enjoyable?*

And.....

> *It was an amazing experience in the days before package holidays had taken off – we had three dirty blue dormobiles – no seat belts of course! – (this was when Health & Safety were not part of the National Curriculum, thank goodness!). We drove from Dunkirk to the Pyrenees over three days, then proceeded via Zaragoza, Teledo, Segovia, Avila, Cordoba, Granada, Elche, and then up the Spanish coast via small fishing villages called Benidorm (!), Denia and Calpe. We stayed in little hotels for one or two nights.*
>
> *Memorable moments included seeing the gypsies dance in the caves near Granada at 11 pm, the Alhambra before many people knew about it, the castle at Segovia, and the Good Friday procession in Avila by torchlight. Also, we remember the vans occasionally breaking down, and an exhaust pipe falling off (not to mention 3 or 4 punctures).*
>
> *Many of Gwyn Arch's "special" choir were on the journey, so there was a great deal of singing too! For those fortunate pupils, this was a wonderful insight into a previously unknown European life, and the travel was memorable to say the least. We had a lot of "races" with our highly competitive teacher drivers – it was great to get to the hotel first as this meant the best rooms!*
>
> *It's never too late to say thank you to those brilliant teachers who organised the trip! (p.s. we named the dormobiles Humphrey, Horace and Henrietta!!)".*

Such self-contained journeys were not confined only to the Continent, the UK has many bright spots to be sampled, one such trip was destined to end up in the Lake District, but not with travel arrangements quite like this!

> *Two-thirds of the party went up by train and the remainder on a hired minibus. One hour up the M1, the minibus died – a blown engine. We spent the whole day at a motorway service station trying to get in touch with people. Eventually one of the students got his dad to arrange transport for the luggage and a couple of the lads to continue the journey. The rest of us came home to wait for the school minibus to return from another trip on the following day. The happy campers that went by train arrived at the Lake District with no transport to the site, no tents, no food and no clue as to what was going on! They eventually got to hear what had happened to us and made arrangements with a local farmer to sleep in a barn full of goslings! We managed to catch up with them the next day and the rest of the week was far less traumatic but no less dramatic. The scenery and the climbs were breathtaking, the cooking was mainly beans and mash as I recall and the weather was lovely. Overall highly memorable!*

In later years, as the cold war was ending and the face of Europe was changing, more adventurous journeys were made by school groups – always mixed boys and girls. Such destinations included a Mediterranean Education Cruise in 1987 – taking in Greece, Egypt, Israel, Rhodes and Turkey – the Soviet Union on study trips, including Moscow and

Leningrad (St. Petersburg) in 1987, 1988 and again as communism fell, in 1990. Berlin, post the 'fall of the wall' was twice explored in 1990 and 1992 and Europe's most beautiful city – Prague – in 1995. Greece had been popular in the late sixties but fell away as the century rolled on. On a downside, a proposed RE trip to Israel was cancelled in 2001 due to advice on security from the Foreign and Commonwealth Office. Such is our changing times!

For enthusiasts of another kind, fifteen members of the Railway Club of the seventies packed their cameras and 'train-spotters guides' and after an arduous journey north on those steel rails spent a week exploring the narrow gauge railways of North Wales, a delightful pastime and interlude in school routine, repeating the trip the next year – destination Kent this time.

For the more adventurous and energetic, the eighties saw outward bound courses taking place in Tunbridge Wells, Kent – a stone's throw from Dorking – a canal trip organised in 1990 around the UK, and a group from the fifth form staying at Stratford on Avon Youth Hostel for a week in 1981, activity unknown! These more adventurous trips were the result of early sojourns in the sixties exploring Somerset, and in particular the Mendip Hills complete with Cheddar and Wookey Hole Caves, and a five day mountaineering expedition in Snowdonia and the Rhynog Mountains in North Wales, armed with Welsh language books. A visit to Anglesey and '*Llanfairpwllgwyngyllgogerychwyrndrobwll-llantysiliogogogoch*' was not mentioned in the tour report!

Sport and cultural visits to Brussels were common in the eighties and nineties, a visit to the European Commission and NATO Headquarters being the feature of one of the visits. With Eurostar now a common mode of travel these visits could even, at a pinch, be made all in one day.

Probably the highlight of physical endeavour was the annual, and twice if not three times each year, sailing trips to the Norfolk Broads. The school's sailing tradition started with the building and launching of the school's first boat in 1956, together with the enthusiasm and management of the late Dr. Ken Smith, and Miss Stephanie Thompson. Not only did the school sailing club forge very close links at Rickmansworth Aquadrome, but also with three different locations on the Norfolk Broads, and groups, of an average twenty pupils, made

Those sailing days
- My boat, my kit, my blazer
- Heave ho – away we go!
- Post sailing 'Shanties'!

the vigil for a week's expert sailing tuition to such towns as Barton Turf, Aldburgh and Potter Heigham.

John Spurgeon, from the fifties music teaching fraternity has vivid memories of the early years at sailing camps:

> *My most vivid and happy memories are not of music at all, but of Ken Smith's sailing camps at Barton Broad, adjacent to a pub with an anomalous licence, where beer appeared through a hole-in-the-wall as there was no bar. The county provided a variety of boats, and I think I must have been the only teacher who preferred the heavier day-boats to the livelier dinghies; their slower, more sedate response suited some learners better, too. In retrospect it was all one long lazy sunny day, punctuated by quaint rituals like "dig new pit" (with the wild variations in the length of the grass as a guide to suitable spots). I enjoyed brief notoriety on the day that two or three boats cruised to Horsey Mere, from where we walked to an utterly perfect and totally deserted beach, where I could not resist a swim although I had no swimwear but my underpants. My wife's favourite memory is of the year when at the centre of camp there arose a shrine to the great god BODMAS which had to be loudly worshipped at dawn and dusk in Michael English's very passable imitation of Dr. Nigam's accent. Later we accompanied (or 'supervised' as the insurance company quaintly put it) the same crowd on holiday in a couple of hired Broads sailing cruisers. Moored up at Reedham, my pregnant wife fell in while moping the deck. Expecting a helping hand or a rope, we were taken aback when everybody disappeared below decks in search of their cameras.*

Amongst the least recorded of trips was the annual sojourn by most of the fifth form of the time and a dozen or so teachers to a youth hostel in Stratford upon Avon, very little else appears on record about these trips, maybe our 'Will' had something to do with them!

As the century and new millennium rolled in, the momentum kept up its pace. An art trip to New York to take in the Guggenheim Museum amongst other sights was followed in 2001 by a visit to the 'big apple' again, but this time for attendance at business studies seminars.

Germany and France remained as popular as ever, culture being the main reason to visit, with Spain coming into the same bracket too.

Field Biology and Geography trips, together with the Duke of Edinburgh Awards expeditions met with a temporary stoppage due to the Foot and Mouth Epidemic in 2001, and in 2003 the school played host to a party of teachers from Italy, Estonia and Romania under the guise of *'European Socraties Comenius Project'*.

Not only were all of these trips, expeditions, exchanges, journeys part of the learning curve in the development of pupils (I know I benefited from those ones in the fifties) but they were academically important, physically demanding, tests of endurance, opportunities to display initiative, and they were also 'jolly good fun'!

22

THE STAFF ROOM

The offer of a teacher's post and hence qualification for membership of the coveted staff room 'club' in the early years was an arduous business to say the least. The interview, which did not assess suitability to 'own' a chair in the room, did ensure however that the best teachers were accepted at the school. Interview technique bore little resemblance to the 'stiff upper lip' ways of early years. Indeed examples illustrate it admirably, to quote:

> *I remember interviews taking place whilst sitting on a dilapidated armchair with a worn Indian Tree Cover, and some candidates even sat on Peter Morrill's lavatory seat to be interviewed. If you stood up when Millie Collings entered the room – you got the job. If you had a beard you would not be offered a post, though several grew beards after joining the staff! One male teacher, on having been offered his post was then informed that it was a condition that he would have to be prepared to help with girls' games. Thinking it might be some kind of test he was relieved that he was never asked to follow the promise through.*

And . . . . . .

> *At an initial interview for a post, with the panel being led by Peter Morrill, proceedings were suddenly interrupted by a knock on the door. The headmaster answered, and left immediately, returning a few minutes later, explaining "I know this is not important to you, but that was a first year pupil who had lost his cap!" To him that was as important as the interview and showed that Rickmansworth School had a child centred philosophy. The interviewee accepted the post – he knew what he was letting himself in for!*

It was worth it…..

> *To survive Peter Morrill's challenging interview at Clarendon School was indeed a surprise. I arrived at Ricky in September 1954 from the environs of Worcester Grammar School for Girls. The almost entirely male staff room at Ricky was quite intimidating (I was a shy young thing in those days!) – but they did manage to wash their coffee cups when I threatened a strike in the Domestic Science Department. One of my duties was to provide teas for the governors meetings on alternate Tuesdays. My pupils were eleven and twelve years old so it was a challenge of their skills, and mine, since the meetings were held in the upstairs library, a long trek from the classroom in those days.*

Those early days in the staff room were relaxed, friendly, happy, but forbidden territory, even for the headmaster. The 'inner sanctum' was a place no pupil could call at, let alone enter, even the headmaster and headmistress knocked before entering.

Pre-term staff meetings were held on the Friday before the new term, at exactly 8.46_ a.m.! At each September meeting the headmaster would read out how to 'deal with pupils', one year an unnamed pupil got hold of a copy of the script. The head was hopping made for weeks. The fate of the pupil is unrecorded, or maybe unrecordable! Other staff memories include:-

> *The head also, whilst descending on the staff-room as soon as the end of the break bell went to ensure that all staff returned promptly to their duties, was also very*

> *concerned about the well-being of his staff. In order to give them marking time after examinations he would undertake to teach the whole school population 'en bloc', which he assembled in the School Hall – for in general – a lesson in German!*
>
> *The staff room provoked interests outside school activities – it was a happy staff who enjoyed badminton and other social activities after school though one member recounts those endless Staff meetings trying to decide "firsts" – the memorable series of meetings to decide which exam board to take!; but above all the camaraderie in those early years both in the Staff Room and among the pupils – the pioneering spirit 'writ large*
>
> *In the early years there were only two female teachers – Thelma Troughton and Stephanie Thompson – they did however keep the female flag flying in a very male-dominated staffroom. Fortunately reinforcements arrived as the school grew*

Staff memories are as important as pupil recollections, more are penned below, all of which paint a picture of general satisfaction at the way the school started, and have over the decades seen that tradition is still upheld, despite quite traumatic status changes throughout that time. Here are a few random examples:-

Staff parties......

> *Domestic Science Department iced a cake, unveiled for the head to cut, only to be faced with a decorated clock face with the hands set to 8.46 _. (See snap staff meetings). He took it in good 'spirit'"!*

Impromptu comments......

> *An English teacher once commented in a staff meeting that the discussion was akin to 'an unprintable act' it might be good fun, but it wouldn't produce anything useful. A few shocked female gasps followed, and then a silence.*

School trips......

> *School trips abroad were relatively new in the fifties – and one teacher recalls being involved in trips to the Brussels Exhibition; by coach across Europe to Rome; and also through France and Spain in a small fleet of Utilabrakes with the Stowes, Gwyn Arch and Alan Hall. In Rome, in particular, he recalls the sterling efforts made to keep the hordes of young Italian males at bay and frustrate their efforts to lay siege to the girls in the party.*

Another staff party......

> *With the party in full swing – don't ask how alcohol managed to evade county council regulations – a certain member of the science department needed to leave early for choir practice at parish church. Departure was impeded, and eventually he attempted to leave via a window; where upon he was relieved of a shoe by a member of the maths department (strange affinity for footwear), he escaped eventually. He later married a young lady from the Choir. Boys will always be boys!*

22 – The Staff Room

Sporting prowess – maybe not……

> *One first year staff member, appointed to teach history remembered in his first year teaching maths to another 3rd year form – which if it didn't do them much good, didn't seem to harm them much either. He also undertook, as did most members of staff then, supplementary sporting duties on the rugby and cricket pitches, sailing at the Rickmansworth reservoir and remembers vividly the staff-student rugby match in which he was pressed into service as hooker – failing to win the ball even once in the scrum – and during which Peter Rowland had his cheekbone stoved in with at least one other member of the staff also hospitalised!*

Official school opening 1956……

> *A great challenge came with the official opening of the school by Lady Mountbatten when we were requested to provide a hot lunch for her and the other VIP's – again in the Library – a long way from the source of cooking but with no gas, hot water or means of keeping the food hot either en route or in situ. Somehow they managed and I think all survived.*

Ouch……

> *One well known physics teacher, determined to take revenge on a notorious maths teacher, wired his classroom door handle to the mains to give his compatriot a shock – only at the last moment to discover that it was Millie Collings approaching the door instead! The end of this experience was never told!*

Morning assembly……

> *Memories still linger of morning assembly when we stood around the walls adjacent to our forms with the hymn singing regularly undermined by that notable maths teacher with his own subversive version of the words*

Smile please – the fifties staff gathering

A no noise rule......

> There was a no noise rule in assembly – staff wore rather solid shoes – children house shoes. The headmaster proceeded down the aisle in pair of old carpet slippers on one occasion, they then mysteriously disappeared from his office one day only to have the head walk down aisle next day in stocking feet instead. Later the slippers were returned – suspect magician – a member of the Maths staff (again?)

Accidents do happen......

> Entering a classroom to see a twelve year old girl (already wearing a plaster waistcoat to support her weak back) fall off a table and land on her head. Amazingly she was not seriously hurt, but I thought she had killed herself. On another occasion she told me, holding up left arm in sling, that she wouldn't be able to do any written work. Her smile disappeared when I pointed out that she was right-handed!

An understandable mistake – (at kindergarten though!)......

> Dave Owen was an excellent craftsman and a true gentleman, it was not therefore his fault that a rustic bench he had constructed for 'Twelfth Night' in 1956 should be standing in the entrance lobby for some weeks, only to be found one day by Colonel Goad, Chairman of the Governors, to have the inscription 'PRESENTED BY THE GUVNERS'.

A worrying moment then – a police manhunt now......

> One member of staff's anxiety (to say the very least) at losing a boy in London after an evening in the theatre. He had run on down the tube escalator and caught the train ahead of the rest of the group. Very kindly the boy rang the teacher's home to say he was ok and sorry, so that the anxiety disappeared when the teacher's wife gave him the message. How times have changed.

An oversight......

> A prominent female English teacher suddenly stood up in a staff meeting remembering she had left a student in detention in her room – locked in her stock cupboard no less – one wonders doing what? Her career prospects suffered a severe dent!

Bang on time......

> A Head of Science loved causing explosions on the school field; however one bang caused students in David Drew's language lab to leap up in shock, pulling earphone cables from their moorings. No wonder he was furious as a result. One can but wonder how Dave Drew devoted his entire teaching years to Rickmansworth School, and nowhere else, after such a shake up.

Camouflage......

> One Saturday morning Barry Kenyon (PE) was expertly assisted in painting whitewash lines (shot-putt circle etc) for sports day that afternoon. As fast as we painted them in

22 – The Staff Room

> the rain, it washed them out. Eventually we retired to the school office to await telephone enquiries. The telephone lines became jammed and the exchange rang up to ask what was going on? Inevitably sports day was postponed for a week.

Recognition of the other kind......

> A certain female head of fifth form, and member of English Department, is remembered and loved by her students for her tolerance and understanding – and for a water-fight on the field with sixth form English A-level students. One wonders which memory is more long lasting?

Does it pay to protest......

> Tom Davies, the first deputy headmaster was a man whose reaction to any grumble or complaint was to roar with laughter, thus disarming the protest

Memories of staff cricket matches......

> Two matches in particular stay in Malcolm Wither's memory; the first when Tom Davies, having gained a headship at Devizes, saw us one Saturday journey there to do battle against his new school. They batted first and he recounts spending the whole time fielding in some non-strategic position on the boundary. It being one of the rare occasions when the openers excelled and he, as tail ender, didn't get a bat. What a waste of his talent and a Saturday, he thought! Sometime later the staff held an evening match against staff of Watford Boy's Grammar School (himself a former WGS pupil) and the bowler in their final over was his one-time science teacher Mr. Wyles. He recalls – I can't remember the exact figures, but I believe Watford scored 100 for 2. Our batting collapsed to 30 for 9, and I went in last man to face the last over of the evening from Mr. Wyles. If I held out it would be a draw (only cricket can camouflage a 100 – 30 defeat as a draw!). By refusing to be drawn and by playing a dour final six balls, even to the most tempting of deliveries, a draw was obtained. My one moment of cricketing glory!

Staff cricket team with Stephanie Thompson to the fore

There were two important occasions in which 'politics' were brought into the bounds of the staff room, both surrounding the changes of status of the school; one to comprehensive in the late sixties, and two to grant maintained in the nineties. Staff reflections on one of these occasions included the following 'incident'.

> In the late sixties, a visit came from a county education officer to 'discuss' the school going comprehensive, a meeting which took place in the very small staff-room. He chain-smoked throughout, back to the wall and by the end of the hour's meeting you couldn't see clearly – many staff also smoked in those days. He wasn't capable of defending what was going to happen, being routed by arguments – but of course there was little point in opposing a 'fait accompli' and the school easily absorbed going comprehensive (to the extent that it did – the academic intake was always very high).

Staff recollections of Peter Morrill and Millie Collings were always popular......

Peter Morrill used to walk round the school picking up pieces of litter, an obsession which, despite his position, he seemed to spend an inordinate amount of his time collecting. I taught in a classroom looking onto the courtyard so all the class could see what he was doing – he would then come into the classroom and announce in a booming voice," I have picked up 23 pieces of litter." Then he'd disappear leaving everyone wondering what to say – most of all me!

Mr. Morrill's assemblies, wandering through the hall discussing the music he was playing – Beethoven's Seventh 'Boom diddy boom boom'. He was so charismatic that the students had no difficulty in keeping straight faces and at the other end of the scale his terrible distress telling assembly about a former student crippled by an accident at university.

A girl with an excessively short skirt was called a 'jezebel' when he saw her outside the assembly hall and the admonition not infrequently given in school assemblies "Jonny Smith broke a window yesterday and I shook him by the hand because he came to tell me about it – long after I will have forgotten about the window, I will remember his honesty in coming to tell me about it though".

He constantly repeated to his staff the maxim that 'A quiet teacher has a quiet class; a noisy teacher a noisy one': it was an injunction which undoubtedly worked (in most cases!). He was always open to new suggestions and supported new projects. I remember the whole fifth year after 'O' levels, being engaged in a kind of treasure hunt/initiative test which involved them, for a whole day, foraging the countryside for miles around to collect various objects and pieces of information.

We were also able to organise, with his blessing, sessions on a Friday afternoon for the sixth form to which we invited outside speakers on often controversial topics – for example, a representative of the Howard League for Penal Reform and the London representative of the Algerian FLN!

In autumn 1957 – the school was badly hit by the outbreak of Asian flu and I recall a point at which around one third of the staff were off work because they had caught it. It was another occasion on which I believe PJTM undertook some mass teaching – in the hall.

Mr. Morrill was a man of great kindness and understanding. His organisation of 'shops' in the hall to familiarise French exchange students with English money were one-man shows which kept large number of youngsters involved, thus freeing staff for the marking of exam papers etc. He was a good judge of teaching potential – five of the founder staff went on to their own Headships.

Miss Collings was an extremely able, friendly and much respected lady. Her performance as one of the old ladies in the production of "Arsenic and Old Lace" was superb. She was an excellent pianist and with Gwyn Arch could often be heard at lunchtimes playing in the Hall.

It was a school with a clear vision and sense of direction. Its 'esprit de corps' was excellent. This was in no small measure due to both Peter Morrill and Millie Collings who though eccentric in many ways, were undoubtedly a driving force

22 – The Staff Room

> who had the well-being of the school and its pupils at the forefront of their minds the whole time. And they were admirably backed by deputy head Tom Davies.

And, throughout these golden years, this summary says probably what the majority of staff members would say:-

> *Pleasures of working in the school – teachers wanted, like adults, to be given freedom to be themselves, and trusted to do these jobs properly – even if they did pop out in free periods to bank or shops, or to the pub during lunch. Students, almost without exception were pleasant, good natured and a pleasure to know and teach. There were lots of theatre trips – probably more than in any other school in the area. Excellent staff relations existed in the staffroom and between staff and head. Annual staff plays, though faded a little in the eighties were revived in the nineties with staff/student musicals held on a regular basis. The staff plays still occur, as well as 'school play'.*

And:

> *The staff were extremely young – even the older ones! The consequence was that we shared a very active social, cultural and sporting life. We played badminton, tennis and cricket together on a regular basis; some of us, under the tutelage of Ken Smith, engaged in sailing and sailing holidays. The staff plays were another symptom of the unusually close bonds which kept the staff together.*

In conclusion – '*a happy staff makes a happy school*' – and the case is proven – '*teachers are human after all!*'

For acknowledgements in respect of the contributions to this chapter, and to avoid naming names where possible in order to "protect the innocent", may I thank all the following former members of staff:

Thelma Harling (née Troughton)	1954 – 1957
Peter Rowland	1954 – 1962
Malcolm Withers	1954 – 1963
Peter Stowe	1954 – 1974
Barry Kenyon	1954 – 1959
Ernie Smith	1954 – 1960
David Drew	1954 – 1987
David Owen	1954 – 1962
John Spurgeon	1955 – 1959
Gwyn Arch	1955 – 1964
John Thwaites	1957 – 1961
Roy Abrams	1957 – 1969 and 1971 – 1983
John Abbott	1965 – 1997
Andrew Western	1966 – 1972
Andrew Daykin	1967 – 1971

23

PUPIL REFLECTIONS

To avoid embarrassment, misery, lawsuits or even another break in my already badly broken nose, I've left out references to any names (where possible!) in the following topical and sometimes amusing stories from former pupils. Names are for you to guess! They show that Rickmansworth School, whilst focusing on providing a right and proper education for all, also had a human side too – both with the teachers and pupils. 'Boys will be boys', an old adage that still stands; and pranks, jokes, mistakes will continue for time everlasting. If they didn't then 'Jack would be a dull boy', and Rickmansworth School would not hold such a special memory to most ex pupils and teachers as it does.

Here's but a few stories to consider, some repeated from my first book – 'The Founding Fifties, A Book of Firsts' – others much 'hotter off the press'. May I, as the author, confirm at this stage that the use of the *'first person'* in almost all cases does not signify that I was involved in any of these often scurrilous escapades – maybe just a couple or so though – but definitely not all!

Geography memories……

> *of a memorable field trip to Malham under the tutorship of, as had been quoted, a good looking Geography teacher. The plan had been to do a study of both a limestone plateau and a river development. Unfortunately for the staff, but not for the students, the weather was so hot that the rivers had all dried up, hence we had to drive around in a minibus looking for water! We got lost, so the Geography teacher, with his Cambridge accent asked directions from a local farmer, and was so embarrassed that he could not understand one word of the reply! He had to ask us for bi-lingual help. We collapsed with mirth.*

And another Geography teacher……

> *who locked himself in the stock cupboard one lesson, as he could not handle the bad behaviour of the boys in his 'O' level group?*

Or Geography classes on April 1st when a few girls……

> *drilled out some chalk with compasses, planted red 'Swan' match heads in them and repacked the ends with chalk dust. We greased the 'dead' end so it wouldn't write on the board. We planted these chalks along the boards of this room during break time. On arrival at our room our teacher came along and swapped rooms – and the teachers! I ended up with him in the other room in the 'booby trapped' room. He struck a chalk along the old style board to draw a map and it spluttered into a spark. Rather bemused he did it with another chalk and it caught fire! There was uproar as he pretended to smoke it like a 'ciggie'. Of course I was sent to the headmistress's office immediately – having been identified as the ringleader. **No-One** got sent to 'Millie' then and everyone thought I'd be expelled. However, the staff had a great sense of humour and went along with it as April 1st tomfoolery! (Luckily!).*

Facing the consequences – or not……

> *on one halcyon day in June we were playing football (with a tennis ball) when, to my horror, I kicked it right through a window, breaking it. I decided to go and see the headmaster to tell him and face the music. I will always remember the scene that followed. I knocked on the door and received the reply 'enter'. Stricken with anguish, I told Mr. Morrill what I had done. He remained seated behind the desk, silent and brooding with a face like thunder for at least a full minute, then suddenly leapt to his feet, his black gown billowing, and descended on me with a gracious smile, held out his hand, shook mine and said, to my astonishment "well done, boy". He was thanking me for owning up.*

Memories of music……

> *When I started at Rickmansworth some bright soul in the Music Department (I believe Mr. Abrams was in charge) had decreed that all first years should learn a musical instrument and to this end had bought large number of violins. Does anyone else recall the excruciating agony of an entire class of eleven year olds simultaneously trying to play "twinkle, twinkle, little star?" It put me off violins for life – one instrument neither of my children were ever allowed to tackle.*

Memories of French……

> *Not being a fan of French lessons, we decided to do our verb test one morning, not on school paper, but on 'Bronco' toilet paper. Everyone co-operated, the test was completed, a few unquotable French phrases were muttered by our teacher, and we re-sat the test the next week.*

And even English……

> *One day during an English class we devised the 'wasp plan'. At one bell, which signalled five minutes to the end of the lesson, we set our morse buzzer off, a similar noise and effective alternative to a large predatory wasp. Everyone, as was prescribed, panicked, chasing around the classroom to try to catch, or avoid the beast. Three bells sounded, the lesson ended, it was over, the 'wasp had been caught'. We all left, leaving our poor teacher scratching his head in disbelief, and maybe not knowing even to this day where the wasp went.*

History – not to be forgotten……

> *The first blushing teacher? Our enthusiastic, earnest (and very young) history teacher was in full flood about Disraeli's wonderful relationship with Queen Victoria when he said "and Disraeli offered her the title 'Empress of India', he certainly knew how to handle Queen Victoria". Of course, we pupils took the alternative meaning for this comment and cheered, with comments like 'what a lad'. One of the girls said 'oh, sir, you're blushing' – and this made him blush twice as fiercely!*

With Maths, also not to be forgotten, but for another reason……

> *The first old crate? During maths one day our teacher went off to his tea break as usual, leaving us to consume the third-pint of milk allocated to us, sitting in bottles in a spanking new crate in the corner of the room. We were on the ground floor and had found a battered old crate in the woods that morning and had left it*

> *outside the window of the classroom. By simply leaning out of the window, we did a quick swop of crates and put our empties in the battered crate. When he returned, he went berserk. He thought we had vandalised the milk-crate!!! He wasn't that placated when we switched the crates over.... but .... Well I don't remember him smiling about it though he didn't demand retribution!*

And practical angles to maths too......

> *Most of my school memories were of being in trouble and trying not to make that early morning visit to the gymnasium as a result! I remember our maths teacher coming to school one day in his hard soled shoes, and by the first lesson, had only managed to change one of them to his alternative crepe soled shoes. So we all went out and came back into his class, with one shoe and one rugby boot on or whatever we could find as our alternative footwear. He was not amused!*

Maths – the easy way – or not......

> *Whilst undertaking GCE 'A' level in Pure Mathematics under the late Dr. Nigam, when doing trigonometry, his words were "You must know this from right to left as well as left to right when studying sines and cosines e.g. $\sin(A+B) = \sin A \cos B + \cos A \sin B$". Also, when doing calculus, he used to say that you must put the "dx" after the integral, otherwise it is meaningless. Finally, he used to say that he could not understand why the class found the problem difficult, because it was so easy. Yes – well!*

And – post script by your author ......

> *Some of his calculus, confused me too! But he was understanding, even when I broke my right shoulder in a rugby match and couldn't write too well with my left hand for two weeks, he accepted my confused squiggles on paper, which helped me hoodwink him into thinking I understood calculus, which at that time I really didn't!*

But with Physics it was always practical......

> *The first uncomfortable moment? Are you sitting comfortably, sir? A decree was announced by the headmaster at assembly. 'Test-tube holders are not, under any circumstances, to leave the science laboratories.' At tea-break the following morning, our teacher sat down on two of them at staff tea-break- we'd clipped them to the back of his long, white coat as he left the lab.' Give him his due . . . . he didn't mention it when he came back – sore about it or not!!*

As it was with Chemistry......

> *One day we made tea in the chemistry laboratory during our final lesson with Dr. Smith, with the instruction that if the Headmaster were to appear and ask questions, we should tell him we were extracting tannic acid. This could have been construed as a 'white lie' had we put milk in too!*

And back to Geography, the primitive way......

> *In the third year as a part of our geography curriculum we were taught how to make maps. One Sunday morning two of us were assigned the task of measuring Croxley Green's boundary roads; i.e., Baldwin's Lane, Watford Road and the*

> Green. Armed with a clipboard and sixty foot tape measure we set off to trek the four miles or so, measuring the whole distance in sixty feet stages. Five hours later we finished. How methods have changed since then.

And what better way to learn map reading – those map reading jaunts......

> It is amazing to those familiar with the modern day caution about lawsuits and liabilities how we were taught map reading in the late fifties by our geography teacher. We were formed into pairs and put on a bus and blindfolded. We then set off to be driven far into the surrounding countryside. Here and there, in obscure lanes, and deserted country roads, our blindfolds were removed and we were dropped off, one pair at a time. Thereafter, armed only with an Ordnance Survey topographical map, a mackintosh, some food and drink and one penny for an emergency phone call, we had to figure out where the heck we were and to find a route to take us back to school several miles away. Contour lines, a ditch, an electric cable line – these were the clues we shuffled in our heads as we tried to make sense of the map. As a last resort you just started walking. As far as I recall, nobody got murdered, kidnapped, run over, molested, or seriously and permanently lost. Some students cheated and hitched a ride or took a bus once they hit a main road so as to get back before dark. Our teachers as they waited for the students to return in the waning light, must have had nerves of steel, or been totally oblivious or just knew they were good teachers. I would vote for the latter. Sometimes it was 10.00 p.m. before the last pupils made it back to school. There's not even a chance that this would be allowed in this day and age......

Sport played a great part in school life, as described in another chapter. There was however the 'pupils eye view' of whether it was an enjoyable pastime, or just plain 'orrible'! The gymnasium was the focal point, as shown......

> The gymnasium – well I hated it, especially when forced to play pirates and basketball against the boys. I believe I am right in remembering that during one pirates session a certain boy left behind mainly flattened girls sprawled on the floor in his determination to win – at all costs? We stood no chance having been totally humiliated before we started by being made to participate wearing our grey school knickers, while boys could wear shorts. Such indignity for us girls.

Was dancing a real sport......

> The compulsory dancing classes in the gymnasium – learning to waltz, quickstep and foxtrot – by being lined up along the gymnasium wall and developing the art of avoiding who you thought were the most undesirable partners, themselves lined up on the opposite side of the gym for your taking – a boys and a girls eye view!!

Sailing was, but maybe not for all......

> As for firsts, two girls were the first to capsize 'Edwina', the cadet-class dinghy that was built under the guidance of Dr. Smith, on a freezing cold day, around Easter time, somewhere on a lake near Elstree, North Watford. They had cycled there and one of the girl's fathers had to come and pick them up to take them home in his work van. One had worn blue jeans, well before the days when the dye did not come out when they were wet. Imagine the state of the car, and her legs too!

23 – Pupil Reflections

And partaking was much more gratifying......

> *The first real pupil-lesson of life? In 1954, there was the 'Stanley Matthews' FA Cup Final. It was fantastic, ending up 4 – 3 to Blackpool, with Sir Stanley Matthews winning the only medal that had eluded him. One erstwhile pupil decided he was going to see every cup final from then on . . . . only to discover to his horror later during the fifties that the school had a cricket match on the same day. So ahead of the match, practice being in the nets, he bowled badly, batted badly and was (to his relief) left out of the team. The Cup Final that year was terrible. A drab game between Luton and Nottingham Forrest . . . . So he'd learnt the lesson . . . do, rather than watch!*

Basketball – the non contact way......

> *I was the first pupil to be thrown off the basketball team, for punching an opponent during a match. So much for non contact sports!*

But the game survived – with expert guidance......

> *The school's basketball team flourished in the later fifties through the expert coaching of Canadian born teacher, Commander Tottenham. Such was his impact that three pupils played regularly for 'Watford Royals', who at the time vied for the position of number one team in England, with one of them subsequently gaining international honours.*

Which always helps......

> *In 1959 the school's athletics fraternity were honoured by coaching help, authorised by kind permission of the Amateur Athletics Association and in the form of British international sprinting champion – Dave Segal – who at the time held the national 220 yards record. It certainly helped the fortunes of those rising stars at the time. Not to be outdone, rugby also improved through the expert assistance of teacher, Dai Lucas, himself a Welsh international trialist. His catchphrase being "never fear, Dai Lucas is 'ere", spoken in his broad Welsh accent.*

Rugby had its moments, in the early years......

> *I remember breaking my shoulder in rugby practice down at Mill End playing fields one cold December Saturday morning. I was duly sent home by bus, unable to lift my arm, but in pain having changed alone in the tin shack pavilion. On arrival at home I greeted my mother with the news that she had to take me to hospital. Rather than sympathise at my pain, she went mad – it was Christmas 'pud' cooking morning and six pots were merrily steaming away on the stove. I eventually made it to hospital and back home, six hours later, and resolved to continue in the game for as long as possible. The 'puds' survived – a neighbour keeping a vigil over them!*

And in different ways......

> *Many of us used to look forward to the annual December outing to Twickenham to watch the Oxford/Cambridge inter varsity rugby thriller. On the bus there and back we sung our hearts out with renderings of those favourite rugby songs, though a little less 'blue' than those sung today. To qualify for the trip one required*

a plentiful supply of toilet rolls, and as much orange peel as could be saved, all for the customary 'throwing of'!

Some more different than others, judging by a second XV captain's report......

As captain of the second fifteen it is my honour and privilege to record the achievements of this macabre team of primeval sadists. We have had, generally speaking, a good season. It is interesting to note that although often matched against older and better players, we invariably lost. The season commenced with a hard game versus the Harvey Road School; and although there was no score we did manage to kill nine of their team, losing only one ourselves. Throughout the season the morals of the team were boosted by immoderate alcoholism and the death of five linesmen. The only game of interest, at least as far as the team is concerned, was that played with the under eighteens from St. Joan of Arc's Convent!!

Even chess had its moments – playing chess against Eton (King for a Day)......

The school's chess team regularly engaged in interschool contests. The drill was for one or other of the teams to travel by bus to the host school who would provide the visitors with tea (accompanied by sandwiches, buns, cakes etc) after which we would play chess, each one of the six team members against an opponent. One year, somehow, our coach – a notorious Maths teacher – arranged for a match against the classiest public school in the area – Eton College. We definitely had the feeling of being the underdogs during an intimidating high tea which was served with great pomp and politeness by our grey-suited opponents amid the polished panelling and silver tea service in our hosts' hallowed halls. When we had finally settled down to the serious business over the chessboard however, the invincibility of our opponents (destined supposedly to be our betters as politicians, generals, barristers and business leaders) fell away as first one then another resigned or was checkmated. We came away with a solid whitewash of our opponents and smirked rather more than usual when the result was announced in assembly the next day.

And awards too......

We used to have a county player (adult) who came to give coaching lessons and set chess problems for the team. The one who solved the most in a season won the prize of a chess book, handed out at year end by the headmaster, with all the other prizes i.e., before the whole school. Mr. Morrill duly opened the book, to read the prepared text by Mr. Smith 'And to Chapman, the prize for discovering the most mating positions, a book on strategies . . . . .' (no mention made of chess!)

No school is successful without the regular practical jokers – the jelly fight in the D.S. Room.....

This disgraceful event occurred after a Christmas party that was held for the fourth year in the music room. In those more innocent times, team games with balloons were very central to the celebrations, and large bowls of jelly accompanied the usual sausage rolls and sandwiches for refreshments. The girls (of course!) prepared the food, and were expected to clear up everything later in the domestic science room. Liquid refreshment was orange squash, but this particular year some cider was sneaked in, and it was a very merry bunch of girls who started the washing up. It began in a small way; a tiny bit of leftover jelly was flicked by one girl at another, who flicked a bit back, then again, then another joined in, and another, and so on, until the whole room was a mass of hysterics and flying jelly. Final clearing up was guiltily hurried, and the inquest the next day was terrible to behold. A large amount of jelly had stuck to the walls, and overnight had dried like bright pink sticky glue. Those girls guessed to be the ringleaders stayed in a break to scrub the floors and scrape the jelly off the walls. One hesitates to name names, even so long after the event.*

I dare you……

I remember first year boys wondering if they had the nerve to throw snowballs at the prefects. No, they didn't – sensible decision.

Practising Chemistry……

Eating mini aniseed balls was a favourite – once eaten you were left with a nice test tube size glass container, complete with plastic lid. I always enjoyed chemistry, and having learnt the art of making 'smelles moste foule' – hydrogen sulphide (stink bombs),I proceeded to charge fifteen of my collection of aniseed containers with the prescribed chemicals, cut holes in the plastic lids, and hid them at strategic points around the school. In due course an order went out from 'above' to call in the council drain cleaners to rid the school of the stench. I recovered the spent stink-bomb containers, no one ever knew.

Practising Biology……

I was the first pupil to empty a large box of live grasshoppers into a classroom – during a lesson – not surprisingly mayhem resulted.

Practical writing……

In the late nineties two ex female pupils, by then well in their thirties, were delighted to see that their graffiti, so delicately emblazoned on the girls toilet was still firmly in place.

And escape and evasion, not SAS style……

There was the 'scandal' of the two boys and two girls who, having crept under the hall stage for some privacy during break, were then locked in by an unscrupulous little prankster, thus ensuring they were very late to a physics study session. The result was an early morning 'PE' session in the gymnasium for the boys, courtesy of the headmaster, and Saturday morning detention for the girls, whose mothers were convinced that their daughters had to attend an important netball match that day!! The fate of the prankster is not known – any admission will be treated in confidence – at a price!

Freshly baked cakes……

Having washed the school 1st XV rugby shirts on behalf of two notable sporting boys in the 1950's, our heroic maiden set about drying them in the domestic science room ovens one lunch time. Besides taking rather longer to dry than planned, the smell hardly resembled that of freshly baked bread or victoria sponge cake, the product of the lesson earlier that morning!

Smells at school – of a different kind……

> *After a particularly long after-hours session of the staff/pupils four-part choir, rehearsing 'The Lady of Shallot', we were all in a hurry to get away, including the caretaker, when I suddenly remembered that I had left my briefcase, and therefore homework, in our classroom next to the library. I scooted up, grabbed it and found myself locked in when I came back down. I made an undignified exit via a ground floor classroom window near the hall and was about to dash off when I was suddenly overcome by one of those moment in life you know you will always remember. The scent of the bluebells FILLED the air and there I was, the only one on the whole school field to see and smell them on that beautiful early spring evening. It stays with me to this day, as do the caretakers remarks, as he saw me leaving. He must have believed me though as there was no interview with Mr. M. the next morning!*

Pupil power-amendments to school rules- list of Points for the attention of all pupils (concerning Before School Break, Litter, Bounds, Lost Property, etc…….

> *Ball Games – should a ball lodge on the roof, no pupil is to climb the nearest drainpipe, or use the map room window, in order to retrieve it. The matter should be reported to the prefects, who collect all such balls after school every Friday. Should a ball be sent into a neighbouring garden, no pupil should attempt to retrieve, but report the matter to the deputy headmaster.*

Changing…….

> *Removal of clothing must only take place in the changing room and bathing in the school pond is restricted to gym periods.*

Escapades overseas……

> *During our school trip to the Continent in the summer of 1958 I remember we all attempted one evening at the Rudesheim Youth Hostel to 'out eat' each other. I ate a bowl of potatoes like the others, my only memory was sitting on the wall for the next two hours, overlooking the River Rhine – unable to move – I'd never been so full of food in my life.*

And……

> *In Zernez in Switzerland, I remember that some of the boys in the party were a wee bit rowdy one night and tried to get back into their rooms via a drainpipe – trouble was they chose the wrong room – the girls' dormitory. They didn't excel in the popularity stakes that night.*

Some special memories spring to mind……

> *I wonder what happened to those letters that were received to commemorate the school's opening ceremony in 1956. We all had to write to someone of distinguished personage, one notable reply came back from comedian, the late Stanley Unwin – not surprisingly for those who would remember him – unintelligible!*

23 – Pupil Reflections

Presentation Time.......

> *Janet Perkins and Brian Debenham, the first head girl and head boy went to London to present the Save the Children Fund donation to Lady Mountbatten at her house, only for her to appear out of the bookcase! A disguised door to Lord Mountbatten's study – shades of Harry Potter!*

Authority.......

> *I remember scaling the heights of pupil authority – becoming a senior prefect in my last year. It must have been good training for my future military career, when having been assigned to early morning door opening duty, I regularly refused to unlock the school doors, even a minute before the prescribed 8.30 a.m. time – despite standing inside watching the poor wretches of lower years standing freezing in the snow, rain, fog or whatever delightful weather was greeting them that day!*

No reflections by pupils, as it was shown with the teachers, would be complete without a few words about Peter Morrill. He featured larger than life in his early years probably because there were far fewer pupils during the build up of the school. Some reflections follow......

> *Peter Morrill was a good educator even though everybody was scared out of their shoes when he got into a black mood. Even when mildly ticked off he would silently fix upon you a withering glare while you waited for the ground to open and swallow you up.*

> *Since this was not something to be wished for, it was possible for Mr. Morrill to take on the task of teaching the entire school in a single class during the periods when the staff were having a staff meeting presided over by the deputy headmaster. He taught, usually, German (not a regular school subject in those days). It included stories about Hamburg, phrases, grammar, and even songs. Nobody in their right mind dared to fool around or whisper, or you'd be the centre of attention of nine hundred pitying stares.*

> *He was firm but fair-minded. He kept items of lost property next to his office and it took a sixpenny contribution to the school fund to get anything back you had lost. I had once lost a pair of gloves that were waiting to be reclaimed. "That will be one shilling boy. Sixpence for each glove. "But, Sir, they are a pair of gloves and a pair is a singular noun, so it should be only six pence" I protested. "Fair enough" he consented reckoning, perhaps, that it pays to regard scholarship potential, or maybe he just knew I was argumentative.*

> *Students playing rugby on the school field can be thankful that Peter Morrill was prepared to put the whole school to work on back breaking labour. During our first year in the new premises, we watched out of the windows as huge lumbering bulldozers and scrapers, hauled by big tractors, moved up and down the playing field-to-be, levelling and shaping the ground. The next task though, fell to us. Before the grass could be seeded thousands upon thousands of stones had to be removed from the surface. We all lined up abreast and slowly worked our way across the field putting stones in buckets before dumping them. Then we did it again the next day, and when it rained there were as many stones as before, so we did it again. Finally, the grass was sown and the next season we tried to play on*

it. You didn't exactly bounce when you hit the ground but at least you weren't lacerated. After one attempt we went on to the Old Merchant Taylor's Rugby Club, not to return to use the school field until the sixties.

Even in the first year at Clarendon School in Oxhey, where we were temporary hosted, the pattern was clear. Mr. Morrill was often to be seen leaning out of his upstairs office window, and castigating in stentorian tones at some misfortunate pupil who had dropped some litter, or punched another student in the head. He had a trick question which he put to you as you stood rooted to the spot after hearing your name roared out as if from the heavens above. "What have you done wrong?!" If you cast your mind back you usually knew what he was talking about – you had walked past a piece of paper without picking it up, or had failed to make the allotted time for an appointment, or were standing in a flower bed, or some such crime. If it wasn't too serious you could confess and go about your business. Not knowing what you had done made you seem stupid, but sometimes feigned ignorance was the best policy. If you owned up to something and it wasn't what he was thinking of, he would say "Well, that too, what else?" And you could end up playing twenty questions in public about all your past sins which he was happy to register but continued to press you until you alighted on the right one. You soon learned, if you weren't sure what he was referring to, to keep you mouth shut. "I don't know, Sir" was the best refuge.

I remember with amusement the story of Peter Morrill taking off his overcoat and putting it over the bonnet of his Mercedes to stop it freezing in winter, as I can corroborate this. In fact I was even taken home in the 'Merc' once, after a school play production when I had missed the last bus. It was a ghastly experience, the car had no heating, on a bitterly cold January night and petrol fumes filled the interior so that I was violently ill by the time I reached home.

However, that wasn't such an ordeal compared to our regular Wednesday morning, 'Headmaster lessons' in the library, (this would loosely be described as general studies in today's terminology). One Wednesday, Peter Morrill, having been round all the local railway stations, came in armed with dozens of huge volumes of railway timetables for us all 'If I was to travel from Crewe to Bristol and back in a day, what connections do I need and what time trains should I catch?' was the instruction. I remember quaking with fear, wondering why he wanted to go from Crewe to Bristol and back, and thinking 'hurry up please someone and give him the right answer'. Luckily for us we were saved, there was always one compatriot who generally knew all the right answers.

With our form domiciled in the wood and metal craft room it was sensible not to go out at break time, instead we would brew up coffee – using the bunsen burners, whilst posting someone on the door to watch out for the odd occasion that the headmaster might decide to check that we had gone out.

On games afternoons during the winter when we were sent out for cross country runs, four of us went to a friend's house nearby, then going better still in the summer when we slipped off to a field off Copthorne Road and sunbathed until it was time to get back to school – panting heavily as if we had been running all afternoon.

23 – Pupil Reflections

For contributions to this chapter, and to avoid naming names where possible in order to 'protect innocent pupils this time', may I acknowledge the afore quoted contributions from the following former pupils:-

    Esme Lane (née Clutterbuck) (56)
    Barbara Picton (58)
    Derek Madden (58)
    Chris Morton (53)
    Dick Chapman (53)
    Janet Crawford (née Perkins) (53)
    Margaret Townsend (née Luetchford) (53)
    Malcolm Pooley (53)
    Trina Chidley (née Goldsmith) (53)
    Dick Taylor (53)
    Tony Midson (53)
    David Hillas (64)
    Carolyn Holleyman (née Rooke) (56)
    Vivienne Kent (née Smeed) (66)
    Jackie Atkins (née Wearing) (62)
    Margaret Heath (née Hayes) (63)
    Bob Jobbins (53)
    Chris Saunders (58)
    Fiona Aucott (née Mackrow-Harvey) (71)
    Marion Eyre (née Pearce) (59)
    Janice Field (née Watton) (54)

24

THE PARENTS' GUILD

There is a strong bond between the Rickmansworth School Parents' Guild and the school itself. The guild, founded in 1963 out of that year's summer fete committee, is a registered charity and consists mainly of parents, any of whom are eligible to be members. Their support is well recognised by the school and at their very first attempt at a Christmas market in 1963 £500 was raised, a lot in those years.

Over the years their enthusiasm has helped the guild to raise considerable funds in aid of numerous school projects, including facilities, equipment and services. Their enterprise has helped enormously with the calibre of education provided by Rickmansworth School.

Such major projects include the swimming pool, the first computer room, a careers suite, the Peter Morrill Centre for Business Studies, opened in 1996 by his son Stephen Morrill, two new minibuses and the new performing arts technology suite, opened in 1994. Added to these major projects have been the provision of new lockers for all pupils, significant improvement in the school's IT facilities, a sit-on tractor for the ground-staff, an extension to the stage and provision of curtains in the hall, a multi-media suite for ICT equipment, refurbishment of the cafeteria and renovation work on three of the oldest science laboratories.

Without the guild's help Rickmansworth School would not be able to exhibit some of the most up to date facilities that support the education system.

The guild meets once a month, holds fund raising events twice a term and sets its goals and pledges for financial support of projects every year. Fund raising events include dances, discos, quiz suppers, casino nights, fashion shows, barbeques (summer permitting!), car boot sales, auctions and an annual 'Spring Fayre'. There's little time for inactivity with the annual fund raising draw featuring prominently over a number of months.

Amongst the guild's annual pledges, are continuing support for both the library and the headmaster's discretionary fund for assisting pupils. The guild sponsors useful services to parents through the school shop, and ensures that the swimming pool, which remains under its own organisation, is available for pupils and their families at least once a week.

All is not work, there is much pleasure in being a 'guild parent'. Sports events take place between parents and staff on an annual basis, tennis and cricket featuring prominently in the warm summers, and the many social events ensure that a happy atmosphere always presides. Without the guild in the first ten years of the school, parents were very isolated from school involvement, probably their only contact was the annual trip to meet the teachers and discuss their offspring's performance. In some cases such events were hardly warming, or social, and the glass of orange squash, or cup of tea, together with a biscuit hardly provided the same atmosphere as now enjoyed by parents. Then that was the fifties style of life! The guild altered that!

At the end of the 'fifty golden years', the school and the guild have produced a bond of mutual friendship and support, which has helped pave the way to achieving the most important aim of the school – to strengthen pupils educational progress.

25

THE OLD STUDENTS ASSOCIATION – THE ROSARIANS

Formed in 1961 and better known as the 'Rosarians', the association started with a flourish. Whilst no organisation existed during the fifties, quite understandably as the first ex-pupils would have been only the few who left in 1958/59, by January 1961 there were enough to hold a reunion dance in that month. Two of the early secretaries, Madelaine Hutchings and Suzanne Moore, helped to get the 'ball rolling'. By the sixties the Rosarians had become an 'arm' of the parents guild, and continued to function with old students sports teams including a badminton, hockey and rugby club – all playing school teams once a season. Car rallies were organised and the Rosa Dramatic Society put on three excellent plays in successive years with productions of "Thieves Carnival" being followed up by "The Matchmaker" and "Hot Summer Night". An invitation into the SW Herts Drama Competition saw Rosa's entry "The Hole" win against strong opposition. Going into the seventies and eighties the association became dormant, no committee, no activities. It was a long wait until the nineties for a revival.

In 1993 two former students of the early years, both members of the guild, Maureen Wells and Judie Edwards set in place the revival of the Rosarians. They managed to build a database of around five hundred names, held a very successful reunion in July, with approximately four hundred attending, and followed it with an autumn bazaar in November. Such was the interest that by the next year the guild fielded a cricket team in a match against a Rosarians eleven. The result was not recorded, maybe chronicled as a diplomatic draw!!

With the one thousandth member, Angela Broughton (1956) joining, it was decided that for the future years, starting in 1994, that the annual reunions would rotate on a five yearly cycle by targeting the decade pupils joined the school. In 1994 therefore this pleasure was bestowed upon the 1960's intake, and 220 ex pupils spent a jolly evening reminiscing. By 1999 the second reunion for those from the fifties had come around again, it was reported that 'Sanatogen' sales were at record levels and combs almost extinct, receding hairlines a contributing cause!

After 26 years, Hugh Forsyth, only the second headmaster in 47 years retired. Fittingly the Rosarians marked the occasion in year 2000 with a presentation on the night of that year's reunion with the 'Red Book' – a 'this is your life' documented history of his time at Rickmansworth School.

Reunions have kept going year by year, and although there was a disappointing turn out for the 2002 event, laid on for the eighties intake, the highlight was the 'Rosarians Golden Jubilee Reunion' on 12th July 2003. The hardworking committee laid on a splendid cold buffet, plenty of drinks were to hand, it was a heat-wave weekend, common during that summer, and approximately 400 ex pupils turned up to a bumper event. Not a scrap of food was left, and monies raised beat all expectations, a donation of which was made to the school to go towards the refurbishing of the science and photography laboratories.

Six of the original thirteen teachers who started when the premises at Scots Hill opened in 1954 were present, and 27 of the founding intake from 1953 made it. In commemoration of the event, Janice Field (1954) masterminded and produced a 'tapestry', interwoven with 55 individually cross stitched contributions from ex pupils and teachers, and which is now prominently displayed in the school.

Rickmansworth School – Fifty Golden Years

The committee meets every three months, holds a database of nearly 2,000 ex pupils and teachers, and specialises in regular reunions, with donations being made to the parents' guild from the proceeds of the reunion. That money has helped provide much needed IT equipment for the school.

Dr Stephen Burton and Marije Ullman help celebrate the Golden Jubilee Reunion, with 400 ex pupils

The Golden Jubilee Tapestry

25 – The Old Students Association – The Rosarians

And the future – preparations are in hand for the 'diamond jubilee' thrash in 2013, and the 'centennial' bash in 2053!

Former founder teachers, pupils and Rosarians enjoy their night

26

'IN-HOUSE' PUBLICATIONS

'*Nisi*', Latin for 'except' (or is it 'unless', Latin wasn't one of my successes at school!) and a part of the school motto 'Nisi dominus aedificaverit' was also the title of the school's first magazine, Volume 1, Number 1, printed in June 1960. Its first editor – Bob Jobbins – later to become head of BBC Radio World Service – (I used to listen to his early morning Word Service broadcasts on shortwave during my time in the Middle East, and enlightening they were too) – was ably assisted by fellow founder pupils Marylyn Robertson, Robert English and Dick Pollard. They opened that first edition with Bob's editorial, to quote:-

The past year may be judged momentous by any standards. Sputniks, space rockets, and Mr. Fl**t's driving test; riots in Korea, Turkey and South Africa, and staff versus school rugby matches; royal weddings have taken place, garden fetes have been planned; and now, after six years of waiting, of careful preparation and thought, in this annus mirabillis, with the school now approaching its full strength, the event for which all have worked devotedly and unselfishly is about to the realised; in short and at last we are publishing the FIRST School Magazine.

The issues of a broad sheet covering the activities of our sporting minority as already published was welcomed, since it left us free to publish a slightly different type of magazine, which we hope you will prefer to the more usual volume of lists and addresses. We hope that future editors will be given the same freedom to print a magazine rather than a propaganda brochure-cum-fixture card.

We make no apology for printing mainly sixth form contributions, since the sixth form, in common with much of the upper school, realising their limitations, and their natural modesty forbidding, refrained from committing their unworthy thoughts to paper. The second year forms were the most prolific scribes and in many cases the most interesting.

It is rumoured, indeed in the best informed circles stated as fact, that the school fund is having financial difficulties. (Mainly because the bi-annual voluntary contributions are dissipated in an orgy of chair rubbers and rock gardens). We the committee therefore suggest, after much thought and deliberation, that (provided somebody else does the work) to raise funds perhaps a school fete could be held. This could be quite profitable.

The editor acknowledges the help of Mr. A**h, whose advice, although not taken, proved very interesting.

But now the deed is done, the fount of wisdom is running dry; the reviled sage will pack his script and leave. (Excelsior! Excelsior!).

The first school fete was held on 25th June barely days after the magazine's publication. It was rumoured that the suggestion had been 'leaked' to the school authorities in advance, but did not rate an 'MI6' investigation!

Nisi was to run for many years, and was eagerly awaited by all at the end of each school year, none less than for the prolific satirical, tongue in cheek observations in the sixties by one certain 'Private Pi' (Form 4Pi, 1963).

The magazine published many poetic, dramatic, satirical and often semi controversial articles, all well edited, and all well written, there was also space for the 'topical' notes, a couple follow:-

> *Recently drivers from the four corners of Hertfordshire converged on Hemel Hempstead for the "Safe Driving Competition". With "experience will out", on their lips and string-backed driving gloves on their hands, each were confident of victory. Four hours later 50 out of the 60 men and all the women drove off sadly chagrined, for they had been beaten by Yvette Abbot of Mr. Heddles form, who is but eighteen years old and has been driving for only a year". (Student Power!)*

> *I hear that the bus to Heronsgate now runs more frequently. The twice weekly return trip has been extended by an extra bus every third Sunday of the month (except in Trinity). What is more, the London Transport Executive has decided to consider our requests for additional "school buses". They suggest an extra ten buses, five in each direction, between the hours of four and five p.m. The unfortunate shortage of permanent staff will mean, of course, that this augmented service will be restricted to Saturdays and Bank Holidays only. (Nothing changes – 2003!).*

The House System

This is based on four houses which form an integral part of school life. They are:

CAIUS (otherwise Keys). This house is named after a local celebrity – "Keys" Capone, a famed locksmith turned criminal. Before being sent up he was officially credited with eighty-nine "through-the-front-door" break-ins in the Moor Park area, and was alleged to be capable of copying any key in under ten minutes. So the house was named after him (Latin spelling made everything all right) and today the house centre is the metal work department . . .

ANSON. So named after an aircraft of this type. The pilot was dazzled by the sun's reflection in the numerous windows of the school and the plane crashed on one of the slum prefabs, damaging beyond repair thirty-one third year sixth pupils and a steam radio.

CAREY (B.B.C. pronunciation of "Cary"). Supposedly the Cary Grant Appreciation Society – in actual fact this house uses it as a cover for subversive activities, such as raising money for the British Communist Party.

PENN. This name has obscure origins. It has been suggested that the name is derived from a certain teacher's one time hobby of bootlegging sixpenny biros across the Herts – Bucks border by moonlight . . .

In the following years other publications were circulated and available at a low cost from the news-stand at the school's tuck-shop. They included '*PSi*', the prolific and satirical observations by the infamous Private Pi in the early sixties; '*Space Age Magazine*' of the late sixties'; '*First Go*', a magazine by the first and second years of the eighties and the lower school magazine of the nineties entitled '*Dogmata*', which itself included topical, sporting and career building articles, none less than as follows:-

26 – 'In-House' Publications

I Want to be ....A Cabinet Minister

The career of cabinet minister is a very rewarding one, open to all those who have reached years of discretion or possibly years of indiscretion. However, for those who make the grade the rewards are high. Average pay is at least four times that of a qualified grammar school teacher and on retiring it is usual to receive a number of directorships in the city – known as "a kick upstairs". Certain qualifications are basic, particularly schooling at Eton, and Oxford. Failure to pass examinations, however, has no bearing on the matter. It is also very useful to have two or three relations already in the cabinet, but most valuable of all is to arrange your marriage with the result that your father-in-law happens to be prime minister. If you have none of the foregoing qualifications, it might be a good idea to study politics – but this is, naturally, only as a last resort. (Never a truer word . . . . !)

All these were very topical, very funny and an integral part of school life. Let's leave with a review from one of them of what might have happened in the succeeding ten years after 1966 and written by former pupil A.J.P. Gould.

1966-76 – The Troubled Years

1966 Britain goes broke as economy collapses. Chancellor seen selling matches in Piccadilly. Croxley Print workers march on London and storm the treasury. Premier makes it illegal to criticise government and devalues £.

1967 Food rationing introduced. Government nationalises farm tractors – Salisbury Plain is ploughed up and planted with rice. Croxley Print workers march on London and lynch their M.P. in St. James's Park. Prices and Incomes Board appear on New London Palladium Show in order to raise money. Sing 'oh we ain't got a barrel of money'; booed off stage. Premier reject U.S. offer for Britain to become 51st state of Union. Opposition deported for criticising Government.

1968 India send food parcels to Britain when Salisbury Plain rice crop fails. Croxley Print Workers march on London and blow up Min of Ag. & Fish. Prime Minister appeals on T.V. for Great Train Robbers to lend him a couple of million. Offers to free the Weasel.

1969 Royal Navy mutinies and joins opposition in exile. Liberal leader declares himself to be rightful prime minister; pirate broadcasts started by paymaster general aboard HMS Eagle off the south coast. Croxley Print workers round-Britain hunger march (sponsored by Milk Marketing Board) a big success. Prime minister continues to reject US offers.

1970 Isle of Wight chooses U.D.I., breaks off relations with Britain. Premier starts oil sanctions. Isle of Man defects to America; is towed away by USS Enterprise and anchored off Long Island. Croxley Print workers run out of strike funds; wreck Sun Printers works.

1971 Entire U.S. Seventh Fleet anchored outside British 3-mile limit. Russia send probe rockets to Britain. TV pictures of the surface of Croxley Moor are relayed to the world (courtesy of Daily Express). Croxley Print workers throw probe in canal.

1972 First black African missionary paddles canoe up River Thames. Central Africa demands return of Britain to constitutional rule. Russians land in Scotland – pitched battles in the street. Johnny Walker's falls to the communists. Immediate surrender of Scotland following threatened changeover to vodka production. Croxley Print workers break into Bank of England, steal £2. 13s. 6d. US embark upon 'War of Liberation' in UK and attacks communists and Scots in north Britain.

1973 Phantoms strike deep into north Britain, bomb Glasgow. Communists withdraw when China invades Kazakhstan. US withdraws when Chinese mission arrives in New York claiming that 'Confucius got there first'. Croxley Print workers blow up Houses of Parliament.

1974 Russia and America join forces to fight Yellow Peril, leaving England to continue war on Scotland. Opposition seizes big chance and home fleet sails up Clyde to tremendous welcome. They promise free whisky for all, sets up government of north Britain. Croxley Printers arm.

1975 Civil war between north and south Britain. King Charles returns from Australia. Prime minister, having sold Buckingham Palace to an American tourist, sends him to the Tower. Croxley Print workers storm BBC and ITV; start broadcasting. After three weeks of showing old James Cagney films resistance crumbles. Governments of north and south Britain fall.

1976 Croxley Print workers take over the country, promise new deal for print workers. New Houses of Parliament built on Croxley Moor; Croxley Green becomes capital of UK.

It could have happened – particularly in this topsy turvy world we live in!

By the late sixties some of the school societies also got into the magazine act and had issued their own periodicals, including 'The Poetry Review' and 'The Scientific Society Newsletter'. Such was the importance of two of the three 'Rs' – reading and writing. Learning English at school is fine; being able to transform it into a 'marketable' commodity is another matter. Production of this multitude of magazines, in ever changing format, keeping up with the 'trends' of the time, was fully encouraged by the school, and enjoyed by all.

SCHOOL RULES – THOU SHALT NOT .....

The 'law is the law, rules are rules and boys will be boys'. From day one in this planet millions of years ago there has been a code of conduct – what is right and what is wrong. Where do we humans learn this? – none other place than at home and at school.

There follows a review of the school rules, exactly how they were written in 1953/4 and how, briefly, they are now, fifty years later. Only seven rules were deemed necessary at the start, these seven continue to appear in the rule books throughout the years, but by now, 2003, accompanied by an additional nineteen new rules. Many of the new ones were developed as the school enlarged, as many such "transgressions" became common place over the years or had been initially overlooked as we started in our fairly straight forward and simple lives fifty years ago before developing into the tangled web we live in now. As you read this, take time to draw a comparison in you own mind of the changes in social behaviour over the years.

Interestingly only one rule has remained unchanged in it's wording during the fifty years, that of Rule 3 Physical Education!

School Rules – as they were in 1953/54

1. ***Absence***
   Parents are asked to send a written note with the child on the day the child returns to school.

2. ***Punctuality***
   Children are expected to be inside the school grounds at 8.50.

3. ***Physical Education***
   No child is excused from games, gym, swimming or showers without a note from the parent. If the child is to be excluded for any length of time, a doctor's certificate should be sent to the school.

4. ***School Lunches***
   Parents who wish their child to have school lunches should send the money (3s 9d. per week) on Monday mornings.

5. ***Homework***
   Two subjects will be set every night. The work to be done will be written down in a special Homework book, and parents are asked to sign this book weekly.

6. ***Personal Property***
   Children are strictly forbidden to leave money or valuables in cloakroom, lockers or desks.

7. ***General Behaviour***
   Children will be expected to maintain, both inside and outside the school, the high standards of behaviour which have been set since its inception.

Rickmansworth School – School Customs as they are now in 2003/2004

Fifty years on, the school rules have expanded three fold to what they were in 1953 with 26 separate rules in all. In six of the above original rules, simple as they were, the wording has changed beyond recognition, even though it still means the same thing, however as noted only one has remained exactly as it was originally worded all those years ago, that is – Physical Education. I'm sure readers do not want to be prompted into an early sleep by reading the additional 26 rules that they spent many years trying not to adhere to whilst at school, hence I've been kind and not repeated them, however if the interest is there I'm sure a copy can be supplied from the school on application! (I'd lay a bet that no reader takes this up!).

Infringement of these rules in early years meant for the boys an early morning trip to the gymnasium for some 'extra PT' courtesy of the headmaster, and for the girls a couple of hours of 'occupational therapy' locked in a classroom on a Saturday morning. Such 'enjoyable' pastimes have in modern years been replaced – the moderates of society deciding that such fun activities should be toned down!

More unusual of infringements included:

'Uncivilised language in a lesson' (bother, drat, gad zooks... !)

'Cutting off some of a girls hair during a lesson' (practice for a future career?)

'Attempting to remove another boy's trousers in the formroom' (he'd forgotten his own before coming to school?)

'Climbing into school without permission' (a keen student in the making?)

'Beating up a smaller boy in the cloakroom' (someone his size may have retaliated!)

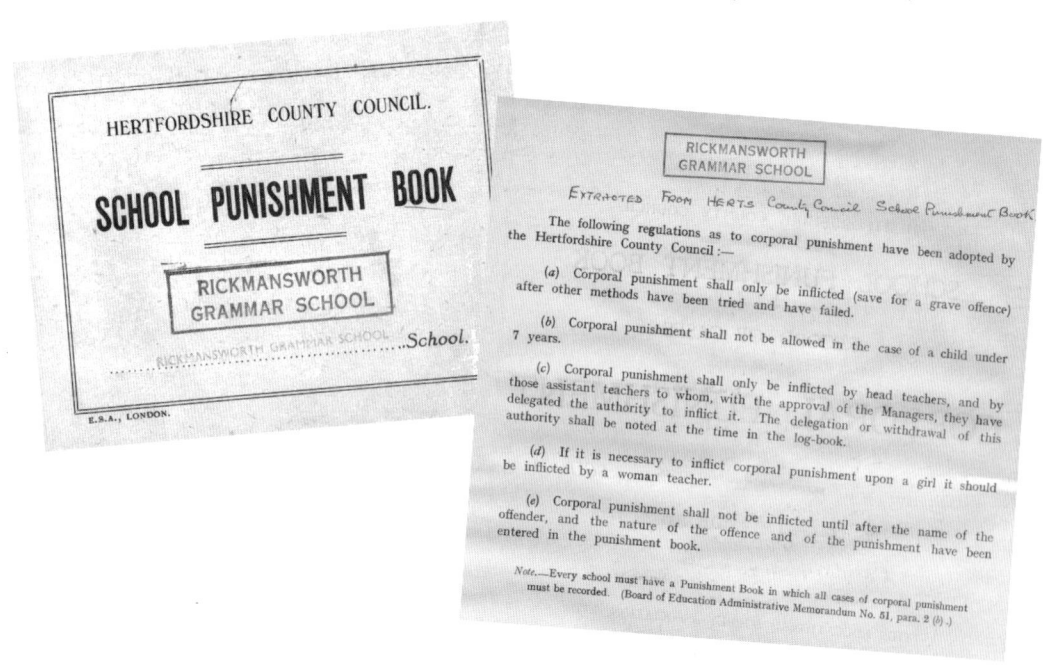

HERTFORDSHIRE COUNTY COUNCIL.

SCHOOL PUNISHMENT BOOK

RICKMANSWORTH GRAMMAR SCHOOL

....School.

E.S.A., LONDON.

RICKMANSWORTH GRAMMAR SCHOOL

Extracted from Herts County Council School Punishment Book

The following regulations as to corporal punishment have been adopted by the Hertfordshire County Council :—

(a) Corporal punishment shall only be inflicted (save for a grave offence) after other methods have been tried and have failed.

(b) Corporal punishment shall not be allowed in the case of a child under 7 years.

(c) Corporal punishment shall only be inflicted by head teachers, and by those assistant teachers to whom, with the approval of the Managers, they have delegated the authority to inflict it. The delegation or withdrawal of this authority shall be noted at the time in the log-book.

(d) If it is necessary to inflict corporal punishment upon a girl it should be inflicted by a woman teacher.

(e) Corporal punishment shall not be inflicted until after the name of the offender, and the nature of the offence and of the punishment have been entered in the punishment book.

Note.—Every school must have a Punishment Book in which all cases of corporal punishment must be recorded. (Board of Education Administrative Memorandum No. 51, para. 2 (b).)

28

SCHOOL STATISTICS

Excluding the very first year when the founding intake were at Clarendon School, it is interesting to compare staff/pupil ratios throughout the latter years, after taking up occupation at Scots Hill.

From 1954, when the ratio, (teachers shown first), was 13/206, successive comparisons reveal the following, in 1960 – 47/880 (still in buildings designed to hold 630 pupils) in 1970 – 66/950, 1980 – 74/990. 1990 – 76/1030 and by the turn of the century in 2000 it was 90/933.

A simple mathematical calculation shows at its worst a pupil/teacher ratio of nineteen to every one teacher, and at its best eleven to every one.

Other interesting – though useless to some – statistics unearth the fact that at the start one third of the teachers were Oxbridge qualified, but by the turn of the century this had dropped to only one in nine from the two 'elites'. However it must be remembered that in the fifties the number of universities bore no comparison to the number that now exist, thought it was believed that qualification for a teaching post in the fifties placed enormous emphasis on where you studied, and quite simply 'Oxbridge' were the winners, particularly if they appeared on your 'CV', if such a document even existed then?

Much importance was placed on health in the fifties – travelling to school chauffeur driven was not condoned, besides which parents' ownership of cars was an 'exception rather than a rule'. By 1960, sixty percent of pupils cycled or were qualified to cycle to school, having passed their Safe Cycling Proficiency Test, and the remaining forty percent had qualified for travel passes – living in such outlying areas as Watford, Chorleywood or Northwood. Times have changed, the once over full cycle shed now remains mainly unused – certainly in respect of cycle storage.

In the fifties and sixties the average teacher age was 28, soaring to 41 by the nineties.

Based on a maximum of 1,100 pupils, 90 teachers and 20 non-teaching staff, all located in 8,500 sq.m. of school buildings, the annual running costs of the school are £3.2 million, or £2,900 per pupil, not far short of university fees, no wonder private schooling fees are what they are!

And finally, the lowest recorded pupil population was 75 in 1953, and the highest recorded was 1,023 in 1974.

EPILOGUE

And so the school was born during global conflicts, Korea, Mau Mau, Suez, Vietnam, and fifty years later still existed surrounded by the same discontent, Iraq, Palestine, Terrorism, Sudan, Rwanda, Burundi.

What will the next fifty years bring as we creep up the steep slope of the exponential curve where technological development sweeps us along at an ever-increasing speed?

Will we see the need for schooling, learning, study replaced by pre-programmed memory chips inserted into our brains that provide instantly all the information and education that it takes twenty years to assimilate by study and development now? Will trains, boats, planes and cars be replaced by 'beam me up Scotty' technology? Will we inhabit distant planets once scientists have learnt how to overcome travel faster than the speed of light? Will we be totally controlled in all our life functions by computers so technologically advanced that they do not bear thinking about now, or will our planet have been blown to pieces by the act of some mindless individual so that we do not exist anymore – then somewhere distant in our universe will it start all over again, a new world, a new civilisation, a new beginning?

Probably not, I guess in fifty years time in 2053 as Rickmansworth Grammar School (sorry yet again – it will always remain 'grammar' to me) will celebrate its 'Centennial Jubilee', those of you who read this book and are around then will look back with fond memories of a school, born out of the devastation of war, and a school that has survived with one *deciding factor* – it is for sure a *'damned great school – one of the best'*.

Regrets to say, I may not be joining you at that celebration – unless I find some miracle age preventing pill – however if it is as good as the Golden Jubilee Reunion back in 2003, then it will all have been worth it.
